Farm Girl

a Memoir

Cindy L. Freeman

ISBN: 978-1-945990-96-0

Published by High Tide Publications, Inc.
www.hightidepublications.com

Thank you for purchasing an authorized edition of *Farm Girl*.

High Tide's mission is to find, encourage, promote, and publish the work of authors. We are a small, woman-owned enterprise that is dedicated to the author over 50. When you buy an authorized copy, you help us to bring their work to you.

When you honor copyright law by not reproducing or scanning any part (in any form) without our written permission, you enable us to support authors, publish their work, and bring it to you to enjoy.

We thank you for supporting our authors.

Book Design by Firebellied Frog www.firebelliedfrog.com

Introduction

Farm Girl, a Memoir is a collection of true stories about my childhood on a dairy farm in Central New York during the 1950s. As I began this project, I intended to compose a novel loosely based on childhood memories. Instead, it evolved into a memoir with a bit of literary license exercised whenever total recall failed me. Recorded as chronologically as memory permits, *Farm Girl* represents the perception of a sensitive, creative, and sometimes lonely child who spent a good deal of time sick and quarantined. Understandably, my mother overprotected me, making me too dependent on her, and my father seemed to ignore me, causing me to think he didn't love me. In truth, he kept his distance to prevent my inevitable reaction to the allergens that he, as a farmer, carried on his clothes. But I don't remember anyone ever explaining that to me. Not only was it inconvenient for a dairy farmer's daughter to be allergic to everything on the farm, including cows and milk, but it shaped my childhood–indeed, my entire life–in ways my siblings escaped.

I pray that anyone reading this account, especially my siblings, will understand that the recorded memories do not reflect how I feel now. I recognize that my parents, who are no longer here to defend themselves, were decent hard-working people and upstanding citizens in their small community of Palermo, New York, where they carved out long, productive lives. Like most parents, they did their best with what they knew at the time. It just happens that they were often unable to meet my emotional needs, which undoubtedly were intense.

I understand that raising a sickly child was challenging. My mother once told me, "You were a lot of work." I suppose she had to expend so much time and energy meeting my physical needs, while raising three other children, that she had few reserves for addressing my emotional needs.

The cathartic act of recounting bygone days through *Farm Girl* has helped enlighten the present and empower whatever future remains. I am liberated by this opportunity to record the memories and deeply grateful for my siblings' permission to share them. I dedicate this book to them:

Marion Loomis Bregande
L. Rodger Loomis
C. Mark M. Loomis

Chapter 1.

Setting the Stage

Farmers don't just work till the sun goes down. They work till the job gets done.

~Author unknown, found on Pinterest

The putrid smell of fresh manure and fermenting corn silage accosted my sensitive sinuses whenever I entered the cavernous dairy barn with its visible beams, concrete floors, and whitewashed walls. The building was cool inside during the summer months, but it felt like a giant walk-in freezer in the winter. This setting was where Dad and Grandpa performed their twice-daily milking chores.

Most days, my allergies to cows, horses, cats, hay, and everything else that accompanied farming, confined me to either my grandparents' house—only steps from the dairy barn—or our house a quarter mile up Route 45. My older sister Marion had allergies, too, but they weren't as severe as mine. She loved nothing more than being in the barn and interacting with the animals. Our younger brothers, Rodger and Mark, were spared the inconvenience of constant cold-like symptoms and oozing skin. As soon as they were old enough to be helpful—seven or eight—they spent the bulk of their weekends and summer breaks helping Dad and Grandpa with the farm chores.

Fifty black-and-white Holsteins stood in neat rows on either side of a long concrete aisle bookended by large sliding doors. Individual stanchions held the cows' heads in position as they faced snow-edged windows in the unheated building. The cow's tails swished from side to side in anticipation of spring when they would need such handy weapons to keep the black flies from biting. The herd fed contentedly on hay that Dad pushed with a pitchfork from the hayloft overhead. The hayloft held hundreds of round bales tied with twine. Cutting the string with a jackknife he always carried in his dungarees, Dad would loosen the packed hay and push the dry winter feed through openings, like trap doors, in the ceiling to the troughs below. During this process, I would have to make a quick exit to avoid inhaling the dust that would prompt an asthma attack.

Farmers, Grandpa (Carlon) and Dad (Lee) Loomis

Beside each stanchion, a water fountain satisfied the cows' thirst whenever they pressed their noses against its metal ring. Chewing and chewing their cuds, they waited with swollen udders for their turn to contribute a share of creamy white liquid to the dairy business that supported two Loomis families in Palermo, New York.

The combined farms spanned some 400 acres of rolling hills, fenced pastures, and a large pond surrounded by dense woodlands. Long harsh winters in the Northeast's Snowbelt were bearable only by the expectation of temperate but all-too-brief summers. With its short growing season and rocky terrain, Central New York near Lake Ontario could not have been a less appropriate area for farming. However, farming was the undisputed livelihood of my father, grandfather, and most families in our rural community. My birthplace was called the Town of Palermo. Still, there was no town—not a bank, library, market (until later), retail store, or government office—only two intersections, one that eventually included a traffic light. The nearest real towns were Fulton, eight miles southwest, and Mexico, eight miles north. Yes, Mexico.

My father and grandfather spent their spring and summer months planting and harvesting crops to provide enough hay and silage to last through the long winters. Mom helped with farm chores briefly after Grandpa died when I was thirteen. Otherwise, her domestic duties confined her to the house. That year, Dad became quite sick. I don't recall what the illness was, but I suspect he suffered from exhaustion leading up to his father's death. Anyway, we all had to pitch in during that haying season. Donning a surgical mask, I climbed aboard the wagon to arrange the loose hay that Mom heaved to me with a pitchfork while Marion drove the tractor. Just thinking about it makes me sneeze. Normally, the hay was rolled into bales for storage, but–although my memory is not clear on this fact–I doubt that Mom and I could have hefted the heavy bales. Also, if memory serves, Rodger and Mark handled

Carlon Loomis Dairy Barn, Palermo, NY

the milking and feeding chores during that period. Rodger was eleven and Mark only eight.

In addition to milking the cows twice daily, dairy farming involved plowing fields, planting and harvesting crops, mowing and baling hay, spreading manure, and threshing oats. At harvest time, Dad and Grandpa filled silos, haylofts, and corn cribs to feed the livestock through the winter. The work was backbreaking and endless. The lifestyle was unglamorous and made me sick…literally. I wanted no part of it. The sneezing, wheezing, coughing, and itching that characterized my childhood were enough to turn me against farm life early and forever. Often, my allergies and illnesses separated me from my father, grandfather, and siblings, creating emotional distance.

On the rare occasions that I ventured into the barn, I would pass by a saucer of warm milk, its steam rising into the frigid air. Each morning, Dad filled it directly from a cow's teat and

Lee Loomis Homestead, Aerial View

placed it on the floor to feed the barn cats, who controlled the mouse population. I waved to Dad who was dressed in dungarees, knee-high boots, and a tattered stained jacket. With his denim cap turned backward, he would reach underneath a cow, his head resting against her ample belly. He was too busy to notice me as he attached a milking machine to one of the "ladies," as he called them. Dad and Grandpa had not always enjoyed the luxury of automatic milking machines. Their thick, calloused hands attested to an earlier era when Dad, his brother, Howard, and Grandpa performed all the milking by hand.

Despite my swollen red eyes and fits of sneezing and wheezing, I wanted to see the weaned calves penned at the opposite end of the barn. There were no bulls on our farm. I suppose they were too dangerous to be worth their value in natural insemination. Instead, the calves were conceived through artificial insemination, a process that traumatized me the first time I saw it performed.

To my dismay, I would have to pass behind the team of mammoth workhorses to reach the calves' pen. Fearing the horses would kick me, I preferred slipping into the space by their heads to feed them carrots or apples. Walking behind their enormous hooves was too scary for a little girl, and I knew better than to ask Dad to abandon his work and accompany me. He had no time to waste in completing his unrelenting chores. Usually, I'd return to my grandparents' house on the property—a home we shared until I was three—to find my petite grandmother cleaning or cooking. I don't remember her ever setting foot inside the barn.

My Beloved Grandma Loomis
in Her Twenties

Across the concrete aisle running the barn's length, Grandpa mirrored Dad's actions with his row of cows. Like a powerful vacuum cleaner, the milking machine sucked each cow's swollen teats and, through short hoses, pumped milk into a covered bucket. The men attached and detached continuously with only four milking machines until they completed the twice-daily task. In large metal buckets, they carried gallons of fresh warm milk to the cooling room adjacent to the barn's front entrance.

A substantial stainless-steel cooler occupied most of the room. Resembling an oversized deep freezer chest, it circulated and chilled the milk until a giant tractor-trailer arrived three mornings a week. The driver would pump the liquid through a thick hose into the truck's refrigerated tank. Then, he transported raw milk to Byrne Dairy's pasteurization plant near Syracuse to be processed for grocers to sell to their customers. Some of the liquid became ice cream or cottage cheese. Some of the rich cream was churned into butter.

Grandpa and Dad in the Milk Cooling Room

Behind the cows, a steamy stinky depression spanned the length of the building. Its function was to catch bovine feces and urine. Later, Dad would shovel the solid waste into a manure spreader and hose the liquid portion out the rear sliding doors into a sewer drain.

A Later Model of Dad's
Allis Chalmers Tractor

The spreader hooked up to an orange Allis Chalmers tractor, which only Dad drove. Grandpa preferred working with a team of horses as his father had. Every day, in all seasons, loads and loads of the fetid mixture were hauled outside and spread on the fields where it served as fertilizer. Turning the grassy or snow-covered pastures brown created a stench that permeated the surrounding air, often drifting into the houses and attracting flies in the summer.

Sticky strips of flypaper hung from the ceilings of the barn and kitchens to catch the pesky insects and keep them out of our food. The sight of fly's carcasses in the kitchen was more distasteful to me than the thought of accidentally ingesting one of the nasty annoying creatures. Perhaps my life-long aversion to milk resulted from more than just an allergic reaction.

My Parents' Wedding -
October 21, 1944

Chapter 2.

My Parents

We never know the love of a parent till we become parents ourselves.

~Henry Ward Beecher, American Congregationalist clergyman
and social reformer

From an early age, I sensed that farming was not my father's career choice, even when the income sufficed to support his family. After all, he had been an unpaid "hired" hand for his father since the age of ten. I once heard him say that Grandpa never woke him and his older brother, Howard, in the morning. He simply expected them to be in the barn by 5:00 am, even on school days. I don't remember Dad mentioning the consequence of failing to report.

Dad was an intelligent, handsome man with a full head of wavy brown hair and intense blue eyes. He had dreamed of earning a college degree–he wanted to study chemistry. But, when Howard went to war, Grandpa expected Dad's help to keep the farm operating. While farming brought Dad no pleasure, he took pride in his trim physique and strong muscles due to intense physical work. He was small for a man, maybe five-foot-eight inches tall and seldom weighing more than 130 pounds. In public settings, Dad was outgoing and friendly. He enjoyed "shooting the breeze" with neighbors, church friends, and other farmers, but, at home, he often seemed angry. His dark moods cast a heavy pall over many family gatherings when he was sullen and silent. When words did surface, they were judgmental and critical. I thought his sadness and anger were my fault. I tried to be a good girl; I tried to be funny and entertaining, eventually earning the label of "the instigator." I tried to be perfect so that Dad couldn't find fault with my words, appearance, or behavior; but overachieving to win the approval of the central male in my life seemed futile. As a child, I couldn't know that Dad's gloomy moods had nothing to do with me. Many years later, I learned he adored me and was proud of my accomplishments. Still, when I was an impressionable fragile child craving my father's unconditional love, his ability to express it seemed broken.

Grandpa passed away when I was in junior high school. Grandma sold her half of the farm, including the herd and most of the equipment. After that, Dad held numerous, varied jobs, including factory work for General Electric in Liverpool, Nestlé in Fulton, and Miller Brewing Company in Fulton. Next, he worked in landscaping. His last and favorite job was with the Onondaga County Water Board as an operator. One of an operator's duties was to test the water that supplied our neighboring Onondaga County, including the city of Syracuse. He performed this task numerous times daily to ensure the chemicals were balanced and the water was safe for consumption. While he worked there, retiring at age seventy-nine, he formed many lasting friendships, and best of all, he got to dabble in chemistry. By this time, I was married and living in another state, but I recall this period as his most content.

I wish I could have understood as a child what I finally began to comprehend as an adult. When Dad was a farmer, he was exhausted, frustrated, and disappointed. The job was relentless and physically demanding. He scarcely got a break from this drudgery that was at the mercy of both the weather and fluctuating milk prices. Prevented from realizing his life's dreams, he suffered from low self-worth and depression. Furthermore, his generation was discouraged from talking about issues or expressing feelings; and seeking professional help for mental or emotional distress—construed as weakness—was out of the question.

Since I rarely visited the barn, suppertime was when I saw my father. My assigned seat at the table was directly across from him. Often, he would sit in silence, his head down, neither eating nor interacting. We would try to engage him, almost like a game, but he was engulfed in a cave of darkness his children couldn't breach.

During one meal when I was eight or nine, Dad seemed angry with Mom, but they didn't discuss or resolve issues openly. I don't think they did so privately either. He began to criticize her, not overtly, but sarcastically when she took a second helping of mashed potatoes. There was a pointed comment about how he wouldn't be able to get his arms around her if she didn't slow down. He laughed as he said this, but Mom, who had always carried extra weight, was not laughing. Her face turned red, her lips pinched, and her eyes glistened, but she said nothing. This was only one of many such interactions through the years.

I wondered why Mom ignored Dad's sullenness and accepted his dark moods and hurtful barbs, even as tears welled from a deep chasm. Because I spent so much time with her, I suppose I internalized her pain. Often, she tried to cajole Dad out of his moods. Perhaps she thought she could balance his blues with her extra measure of cheerfulness. But I came to realize Dad was in pain from his own unresolved issues.

Dad's Diaries

My dad kept diaries;
I never knew why.
I read some entries after his death.
Dates, facts, weather reports.
Devoid of emotion, commentary, critique—
no words to reveal who he was or how he felt.
I would like to have known the man inside.

His journals were like him—
afraid to go there;
too much pain, too broken,
furiously paddling to stay afloat;
existing on the surface
where sunlight masked darkness.

I wish I'd understood his anger and sadness.
It's too late.
I berate myself for not pressing harder.
Yet, I know the wall was solid, immovable, nonporous.
I wonder why he kept those diaries,
a mystery for all time.
Perhaps, like me, he just needed to write.

Mom would build up Dad to his kids as if he were a god. I suppose it was her way of defending his behavior. I found it confusing. Instead of holding him accountable, she'd excuse his critical comments, saying things like, "He doesn't mean it" or "He doesn't speak to me like that in private."

When I was a teenager, I remember thinking, *Why doesn't she stand up for herself? Why does she walk away and cry in private instead of telling him to knock it off?* To this day, I wonder if he even realized his words were hurtful. I don't think he intentionally lashed out at the woman he supposedly loved for sixty-five years. Rather, I think he was hurting from his own unresolved issues and needed to vent.

Yet, this emotional dance wasn't the summation of their relationship. There were times my parents' love for each other shone brightly. I remember watching Mom freshen her lipstick and hairstyle just before Dad came in for supper. Often, they groomed each other while attending functions, straightening a lapel, or patting a loose strand of hair into place. In the evening, they would sit on the sofa holding hands as they watched *Gunsmoke* or *Bonanza*. Years later, there were Mom's numerous surgeries, after which Dad cared for her. During one of her many hospitalizations, I remember watching as he tenderly tucked the covers around her shoulders. The act struck me as both sweet and surprising.

Stone Fireplace Built by Dad

Even as Dad held other jobs, there was much work on the homestead property: mowing, pruning, weeding, maintaining a large garden, and removing snow in the winter.

While I was away at college, Dad built a beautiful stone fireplace in the living room, hauling rocks from one of the meadows and splitting every stone himself.

In addition to the wood furnace in the cellar, the fireplace created a nearly full-time job of felling trees, hauling logs, and chopping and piling stacks and stacks of wood. He became compulsive about this self-imposed task. Throughout his youth, he had been accustomed to hard physical labor, perceiving himself as lazy unless he was straining his muscles to the limit. Incomplete tasks weighed heavily on his mind, and he would sometimes joke that he had to go to work at the water board to get some rest. Yet, because he enjoyed gardening and craved sunshine, he voluntarily assumed many landscaping duties of the water board's property while working there.

Mom also held many jobs through the years, her least favorite being a brief but grueling night job at the Sealright factory in Fulton when I was four. Mostly she worked as an executive secretary at General Electric in Syracuse, but when GE closed, she became a sales representative for a life insurance company.

With the help of my parents, plus scholarships and student loans, I earned my music education degree at a private college far away in North Carolina. I will always be grateful to them for facilitating that life-altering experience.

Dad protected his income with extreme frugality, pouring over the *Wall Street Journal* daily and making many wise—and some unsuccessful—investments throughout his lifetime. Despite his humble beginnings, he amassed a sizable nest egg and never needed to own a credit card. Instead, he paid cash for everything, including cars.

My parents lived in the same house for forty-five years, renovating it inside

My Childhood Home after Renovations

and outside more than once. Still, Mom always hoped to build the dream house she had designed in her high school home economics class. As usual, Dad was reluctant to spend the money. He finally agreed under duress but insisted the new house must include a full basement and three-car garage to store all his tools, vehicles, and collections.

Mom and Dad were in their seventies when they rented out the homestead house and moved into their beautiful new ranch-style home on an adjoining part of the property. Despite his initial hesitation about starting the project so late in

Mom's Dream House Built After Forty-Five Years of Marriage

life, Dad enjoyed watching every aspect of the construction process. They lived there for nearly twenty years. Although they paid cash for their new house, they still left generous bequests to their four children and supported their favorite causes. The gratitude for my inheritance is tinged with sadness that my father never felt worthy of enjoying the fruits of his hard labor.

From my father, I gained frugality, a strong work ethic, and a passion for reading and writing. An avid reader and daily journalist, Dad could write a speech worthy of political campaigning. Peppered with jokes plagiarized from his stockpile of *Reader's Digests*, Dad's talks could captivate our mutual high school alumni association or the congregation of Palermo United Methodist Church. He proudly helped erect its new building when the congregation outgrew its tiny country church at Upson's Corners.

From my mother, I gained a love of music, especially singing, and an appreciation for all things beautiful. My mother instilled in me a reverence for God. Her Heavenly Father was her constant companion throughout life. Although her God of my childhood manifested more as a morality cop than a loving Father, I came to appreciate that she took seriously her responsibility to "train up [her] child[ren] in the way they should go (Proverbs 22:6)."

Before Mom's brain surgery in her sixties, she often served in leadership positions in her church and community. The surgery to remove a benign tumor left her with aphasia and balance issues, challenges that plagued her for the remainder of her life. After extensive physical, speech, and occupational therapies, she regained much of her speech but suffered repeated falls resulting in multiple broken bones and hospitalizations. Despite these myriad physical ailments, she lived to the age of ninety-three.

Palermo United Methodist Church that Dad Helped Construct

My parents were married sixty-five years. I wrote a poem for their sixtieth wedding anniversary and framed it for them. It was time to let go of any past resentments and express my gratitude for their many sacrifices.

Ode to My Parents

I entered the world in '49, the eighth day of May.
How appropriate that my birth occurred on Mother's Day!

You held me, rocked me, sang to me; you took me home to stay.
You raised me with your loving care amid the cows and hay.
You diapered my bottom and wiped my nose.
you read and cuddled and sewed my clothes.

You gave me your faith, work ethic, and love,
while seeking His guidance from above.
You cared for me in sickness and health.
You filled me with music and shared your wealth.

You scrimped and saved and went without,
believing in me without a doubt.
You sent me to college in search of my dreams
of singing, conducting, and teaching, it seems.

I've lived a great life, overflowing with joy,
with a loving husband, a girl and a boy;
my precious grandchildren, friends I hold dear,
abiding faith, a fulfilling career.

As I enter my golden years, a lifetime has already passed,
but I look forward, never behind, for life is still such a blast!
It's just the beginning, not the end. We'll meet in heaven one day,
where you'll be waiting with open arms to, again, show me the way.

You gave me all you possibly could. I'm grateful to each of you
for loving, caring, forgiving, sharing, and patience as I grew.
I love you more than words can say. I know you love me too.
With gratitude, I dedicate this poem to both of you.

Chapter 3.

A Child's Curiosity

Yes, Virginia, there is a Santa Claus.

~Francis Pharcellus Church, American publisher, editor, and author.

I have no memory of the following event, but my mother related it to other people and me through the years. Mom said it happened on a rare, sunny December day when I was three. A fresh layer of fluffy snow covered the ground, concealing the muddy brown patches of earth usually exposed by passing snowplows.

My sister, Marion, had just boarded the bus for kindergarten, and Mom was tending to our baby brother, Rodger, in another room. She told me it always reassured her to hear me talking or singing to myself. Whenever she detected my constant chatter, she knew I was playing safely and happily nearby. On this occasion, it sounded like I kept repeating the same question, something about Santa. Perhaps Mom thought I was reciting my Christmas list to the plastic Santa that decorated our living room wall. Undoubtedly, the winter of my third year brought my first real awareness of the "big guy" and his significance.

Upon finishing with my brother, Mom entered the room to find me, still in my footed pajamas, standing on a chair and peering out the large front window of our farmhouse, my nose pressed to the icy glass. I kept asking, "Where are all the Santa Clauses?"

"What are you talking about?" Mom inquired as she reached for me. "Climb down from that chair before you fall." Had I toppled to the right, I would have landed in the center of our fully trimmed Christmas tree. Tipping in the opposite direction would have meant crashing onto the hardwood floor with no pine boughs to break my fall.

According to my mother, I resisted her arms and turned to face her with questioning eyes. I pointed a chubby finger at the snow-blanketed yard, asking again, "Mommy, where are all the Santa Clauses?"

"What do you mean, honey? There's only one Santa Claus. He'll come soon, but not today." Grasping the back of my pajamas, she moved closer to the window to see what prompted my curiosity. Pointing to something beyond the windowpane, I posed my question again, this time with frustrated-toddler insistence. "Mommy, where are all the Santa Clauses?"

When Mom looked out the window to gaze upon the sparkling wintry tableau, finally, she understood. In the front yard of our property stood dozens of deer with large, brown eyes and thick winter fur, some with massive antlers. Brazenly, they foraged on the frozen evergreens, but there wasn't a Santa Claus in sight.

Christmas 1956 - Loomis "Stairsteps"
Mark, Rodger, Me, and Marion

Chapter 4.

The Life of a Farmer's Wife

Well, farmers never have made money. I don't believe we can do much about it. But of course, we will have to seem to be doing something; do the best we can and without much hope. The life of the farmer has its compensations, but it has always been one of hardship.

~Calvin Coolidge, thirtieth president of the United States

At the age of four, I still slept in a hand-me-down crib in a cramped bedroom on the first floor of our old farmhouse. With the overnight babysitter, Marion shared a double bed, squeezed tightly against my crib. Our bedroom had no closet, only a chest of drawers that partially blocked the window. To this day, I wonder how all that furniture managed to fit into a room no larger than a walk-in closet. The twelve-year-old babysitter came at bedtime and stayed until noon the next day, allowing Mom to get some sleep before returning to her temporary night job. While Mom's night work was short-lived—one summer, I think—providing an additional source of income during a lean year, it had a lasting impact on me. I missed her tucking me in and worried she wouldn't be there if I had an asthma attack in the middle of the night.

Throughout the winter months, the sky remained overcast, and snow fell almost daily, piling higher and higher. Our hundred-year-old house was cold in the morning until Dad fed the wood-burning furnace in the cellar and the mammoth iron cook stove in the kitchen. It would take an hour for precious heat to rise through an exposed metal pipe, at last filling the house with warmth. We slept with the windows open in the summer, allowing a pleasant breeze to cool us and carry the comforting night sounds of frogs and distant foxes into our bedrooms. But in the winter, we might awaken to windows edged with snow… on the inside.

Sometime during my childhood, Dad turned the unfinished second floor into two large bedrooms. I wonder how he found the time while working from dawn until suppertime to keep the fires burning, feed and milk the herd, clear the driveway of its incessant white blanket, and maintain farm equipment. Sometime, when we were older, Marion and I moved upstairs where, at last, we could enjoy a bit of space and privacy. We even had a closet.

Instead of a soft Teddy bear, I hugged a nameless, vinyl-covered elephant at

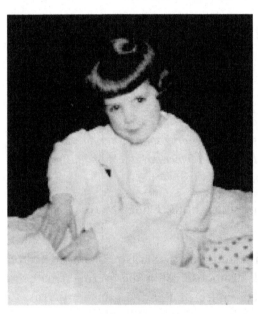

1952 at Age 3 with
My Vinyl Polka-Dotted Elephant

night. Since I suffered from allergic eczema and asthma, there were no furry, cuddly stuffed animals for me! They retained dust and pollen that could exacerbate my allergic condition. Nor could we keep indoor pets. Cats and dogs lived on the farm but stayed outside, finding shelter in the barns and outbuildings.

During Mom's night job at the Sealright, a container factory in Fulton, I remember waking to muffled chatter floating from the kitchen at the opposite end of the house. With my elephant companion wedged under my arm, I scrambled out of the crib, and, stepping across Marion's bed, headed for the kitchen where the stoked wood-burning stove burst with warmth and coffee perked in a large metal percolator. Even in the summer, our house might be cool enough before sunrise to require a fire.

The only part about Mom's nighttime job I liked was when the three other women from her carpool stayed for coffee and homemade fried cakes—otherwise known as donuts. Mom didn't allow me to eat sugar because it caused my skin to itch. She knew the itch wouldn't go away until I scratched my hands and arms raw, replacing one unpleasant sensation with another. But I could ingest plain fried cakes without the powdered sugar coating.

Often, Mom would share her story of how I nearly died in infancy because of my uncontrollable allergies. According to her, I was allergic to every food she introduced, including cow's milk. I was also allergic to cows, hay, oats, pollen, ragweed, horses, dogs, cats, and my father and grandfather, who carried all those odors and dander on their clothing. A simple hug from either of them could send me into a violent asthma attack. Whenever that happened, Mom would make a tent over my bed with a sheet, turn on the steam vaporizer, and cover my chest with a mustard plaster. Sometimes it relieved my symptoms, but other times, I lay awake gasping for breath and wishing I could close my eyes and never wake up. Breathing was too much effort.

Occasionally, Mom and Dad would have to rush me to the doctor in Fulton for an injection.

After much experimentation and failure, fearing I would die of malnutrition, Mom discovered I could tolerate goat's milk. That's when she bartered with a local goat farmer to exchange a daily supply of cow's milk for his goat's milk.

I also underwent regular sunlamp treatments for my eczema. A doctor in Fulton treated my raw, broken skin with exposure to artificial UV rays. He would send us home with a tar mixture to spread on my open wounds. Covering them with gauze was supposed to keep the black salve from staining my clothes and bed linens. Wrapping my hands with clean, white socks was intended to keep me from scratching the terrible itch. Nothing worked.

Marion, Age 2, and Me, 6 Months,
Covered in Eczema

Early each weekday morning throughout Mom's night-job period, four bone-tired women slumped at the large table in the center of our kitchen while it was still dark outside. Dad had already left for the barn to accomplish his morning chores. Soon, Marion and I were sipping mugs of hot velvety Postum, a yummy grain beverage. While the babysitter checked on our sleeping brother, we eavesdropped on the stories of weary young mothers at dawn—women who worked in a factory until 5:00 am, returning home after their farmer husbands had left for the barn. Next, the women fed and clothed their children, prepared meals for the day, and slept until noon while someone else cared for their broods. They spent their few waking hours cleaning, washing clothes for large families, and working in vegetable gardens until it was time to return to the factory.

It was the only way to make ends meet during the unpredictable lean years characterizing farm life. Although Mom's night job lasted only a few months, we were relieved when it ended, especially me.

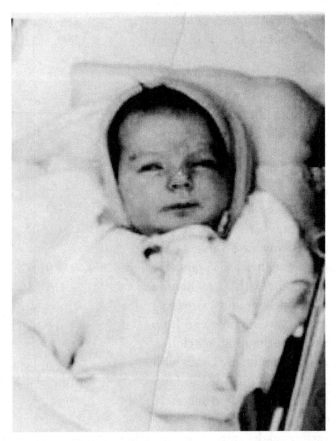

Me at 3 Months.
Notice My Sock-Covered Hands.

Chapter 5.

Mom Enters a Contest

Life's under no obligation to give us what we expect.

~Margaret Mitchell, American novelist and journalist whose only novel was Gone with the Wind

One evening in the summer of 1954, Marion and I accompanied our mother to a Ladies Home Bureau (LHB) event at the Grange hall. The LHB was a group of farmers' wives who met monthly to make crafts, share homemaking tips, learn new skills, and perform service projects. I had just turned five and would be starting kindergarten in the fall. Mom, an expert seamstress, had entered a sewing contest sponsored by the LHB. She created a lovely frock to model for a panel of judges. Mom made most of our family's clothes on her Singer sewing machine, working the treadle up and down with her foot like a pump organ. She was so accomplished that she made wedding gowns and tailored suits for friends and neighbors.

Mom spent weeks designing her original creation by combining elements from numerous Simplicity and McCall's patterns. I watched her spread wispy pieces of paper on the dining room table, and, with straight pins, she affixed them to the pretty fabric she had selected. Muted pink and yellow flowers with green leaves swirled together in a motif that reminded me of the modern art paintings

I had seen in books.

The bodice panels crisscrossed in front, meeting in the back where a large button, covered in matching fabric, held them in place. Mom lined the sections before attaching them one by one to a flowing skirt with wide pleats and pockets. Whenever I observed the meticulous process, I watched her iron every seam until it lay flat. Then she hand-stitched the raw edges, assuring that the inside of the dress looked as finished as the outside. Each time she added a section by stitching the pieces together, she would try on the new combination to ensure it fit her plump, well-proportioned frame.

Finally, the evening of the anticipated event arrived. Confident that my mother would be declared the winner, I grew excited about attending the fashion show. As she flitted about, her face pinched in concentration, she pressed her dress with a new steam iron then stored it carefully in a paper dress bag. After packing the appropriate hat, shoes, and jewelry to accessorize her masterpiece, she announced she was ready to go.

1957 - Mom Wearing Her Contest Dress

Keeping Rodger with him, Dad dropped us off at the Grange building. When we entered the bustling hall, we could feel the contestants' excitement as they darted in and out of temporary dressing rooms along the rear wall. Mom slipped behind a curtain, instructing Marion and me to stand just outside because she would need help buttoning the back of her dress, and someone would need to check that her hosiery lines were straight. When our mother emerged, I remember how beautiful she looked in her elegant ensemble, including white gloves, white pumps, a straw purse, and a white hat.

I jumped when, over a loudspeaker, a woman's booming voice announced, "Fifteen minutes, ladies! You have fifteen minutes! All children should go upstairs now!"

Wait! What? Nobody told me I wouldn't be staying with my mother. I thought I would be allowed to watch the fashion show. Not one to like surprises, at the age of five, I didn't appreciate a surprise involving strangers and separation from my mother.

"You girls run along now," Mom said. "Go upstairs with the other kids."

"But I don't want to go. I want to stay with—" I tried to protest, but Mom's shaky hands and shallow breathing told me she was too nervous about the contest to be patient with her insecure five-year-old.

She said, "Marion, take your sister's hand and go upstairs," her voice trembling. Before I could finish my complaint, a bossy woman in an ugly brown suit interrupted and ushered us brusquely to the enclosed stairwell. Mom always wore cheerful colors like bright pink, deep yellow, and royal blue, making brown seem dull and unappealing to me. I started to cry, but Mom was too distracted to notice, and the bossy woman was unmoved by my distress.

Once upstairs, the brown-suited woman ushered us into a long narrow, windowless conference room with folding chairs arranged in neat rows. At one end of the room, someone had cleared the wall of pictures or plaques as evidenced by rectangles of darker paint dotting the wall. I had never seen a movie and didn't know what to expect.

Then the lights went out. I was afraid, not only because of the dark, but since I hadn't started school yet, I didn't know the other children. Marion left me and sat in the back row with some of her friends. I wished I could sit with her, but, in the darkened space, I was afraid to move and concerned if I joined her group, they would reject me.

Behind me, a movie projector lit up and sputtered before throwing colorful images onto the makeshift movie screen. A white-haired Black man named Uncle Remus appeared and introduced a show called *Song of the South*. It was larger than life and in color, no less! In the 1950s, no Black people lived in my small rural community, so Uncle Remus was the first adult person of color I had ever seen. I watched the little boy, Buckwheat, on *Spanky and Our Gang* but had never met a real Negro (as Dad called them).

Uncle Remus seemed friendly, intelligent, and talented, and he was kind to the children, both Black and White. I remember thinking I'd like to meet him one day, sit at his feet to listen to his stories, and sing and dance with him.

The movie held me spellbound for more than an hour. Not once did I think about the fashion show I was missing. Soon, I abandoned my fears, losing myself in the enchanting stories of Brer Rabbit, Brer Fox, and Brer Bear with their zany adventures in the Briar Patch. When the film ended, I was singing along to "Zip-a-dee-do-dah." I couldn't wait to tell my parents about it.

When Dad picked us up from the event, Mom seemed sad. As Marion and I climbed onto the backseat, I wanted to describe the movie to my parents, but I thought it best to keep quiet. I sensed I shouldn't mention the sewing contest or the fashion show, but my ever-outspoken sister blurted out, "Did you win the contest, Mom?"

Still wearing her stunning dress, our mother slipped into the passenger seat, trying to hide her glassy eyes. She answered meekly, "Second place." Now glancing toward Dad, her face as pink as her hat, Mom appeared more embarrassed than sad. I didn't know what to say. I could tell the contest had meant a great deal to her, and I thought her dress was lovely. Her sewing ability, admired by friends and family far and wide, had been a source of pride for many years. I thought Dad should put his arm around her and draw her close. I wondered why he didn't utter words of encouragement or comfort. Perhaps he didn't know what to say, either.

Mom continued to sew our clothes and even made my senior recital gown and exquisite wedding gown and veil many years later, but she never again entered a sewing contest. As I recall this incident, I wonder why she didn't win.

Was her dress too modern in style or perhaps not trendy enough? Was she penalized because of her full figure? Did she fail to follow the rules of the contest? Was it rigged in favor of the town commissioner's wife or the school superintendent's wife? Mom is gone now, so I'll never know the answers to my questions.

What I know for sure is that my mother was an excellent seamstress. I still have my lovely custom-designed wedding gown and veil as evidence of her skills.

1972 - My Beautiful Wedding Gown and Veil
Designed and Sewn by Mom

Chapter 6.

School Days

If I cannot fly, let me sing.

~Stephen Sondheim, American composer and lyricist of musical theater fame

I wanted to go to school like my sister instead of staring out the window as she boarded the bus. At the same time, I feared leaving my familiar predictable world. I was timid and still dependent upon my mother, who overprotected me because of my frequent illnesses.

I wondered what the inside of the school bus looked like and how it felt to ride the giant yellow contraption. I could only imagine how the seats felt, how it smelled inside, and whether I'd be tall enough to see out the windows. As Marion climbed the steep steps each morning and disappeared for the day, I wanted to carry books and be assigned homework like her. However, at four years old, I had another whole year to wait. I would need to devise creative ways of entertaining myself since Mom was always busy with housework, cooking, and caring for my two-year-old brother.

Some mornings after the bus pulled away, I played school. Of course, I was the self-appointed teacher. My little brother didn't follow directions well, so the dolls I lined up on the living room sofa served as my pupils. I named my favorite doll Darlene. She had long shiny brunette hair that I loved to brush and style, adding colorful ribbons left from Mom's sewing projects: a red ribbon to match one dress or blue to coordinate with another. I was especially fond of long hair because Mom kept my hair cut in a short pageboy with precise straight bangs. I'm sure it was easier for her to maintain and less prone to irritate my "eczemic" oozing skin. I brushed Darlene's hair so much that, before long, most of it fell out, but even bald Darlene was unique because I could make her walk. Her stiff legs moved in response as I maneuvered her arms back and forth. Hip joints allowed her to sit, but she never learned to sit correctly because she lacked knee joints. Instead, her legs stuck out straight. No matter. She was a good listener.

My Betsy Wetsy doll looked like a miniature baby. She had arrived on my birthday, along with a cardboard suitcase of extra clothes, including tiny cloth diapers. She would wet her diaper whenever I fed her water from a plastic bottle. Like most mothers, I grew tired of changing her, but instead of engaging in potty training, I stopped feeding her. Problem solved. My bedtime companion completed my classroom lineup: a nameless, vinyl-covered elephant with red polka dots.

I "read" to my pupils, who adored me, following my instructions without hesitation or complaint. Whenever I played school with Marion, she wouldn't allow me to be the teacher, and I didn't like being my sister's pupil. She grew impatient with me for not comprehending her first-grade curriculum and teased me for holding books upside down when I pretended to read. Typically, I'd storm out of her classroom in a huff, accusing her of being a mean teacher.

***

The following September, I was finally old enough to ride the school bus, but such a brief trip scarcely afforded me the chance to sit before reaching my destination. The distance from my family's farmhouse on top of the hill to my elementary school at the bottom was less than a half-mile, making us Loomis kids the final passengers to board.

On my first day of kindergarten, Marion and I waited at the end of the driveway. As soon as I spotted the bus rounding the bend in front of Grandpa's barn, I wanted to turn and run back to the house. My stomach flip-flopped in anticipation of the unknown adventure awaiting me. There was no kindergarten orientation to prepare anxious children for their first day of school in those days.

My mother stood on the front porch holding my brother and waving encouragingly. I didn't realize it then, but she was pregnant with my youngest brother, born the following February. Mom called to me, "It's okay. You'll be fine," but I read the worry in her eyes. Then she instructed my sister to hold my hand and help me up the steps.

When the bus stopped at our driveway, its brakes squealing, I realized there was no turning back. Tears tried to well in my eyes. I swallowed hard, pretending to be brave. The hinged door opened with a squeak, and I looked up to see the kind eyes of Mr. Baldwin, a large man whose wide girth spilled over the edge of the driver's seat. Marion took my hand and helped me climb the steep steps. I was carrying a shiny new Mighty Mouse lunch box and wearing a blue and white polka-dotted dress that Mom had made for my first day of school. For once, she had not dressed Marion and me like twins.

"Well, good morning, ladies," Mr. Baldwin greeted in his friendly voice.

First Day of School

"How are we today?" I watched him wave to my mother before closing the door by pulling a giant lever. I avoided eye contact with the other children as Marion pushed me along the aisle and found an empty seat. I had convinced myself that the other passengers were experienced bus riders who could sense my anxiety. I climbed onto the green vinyl-covered bench and sat back, but my legs didn't reach the floor. They stuck out straight like bald Darlene's as if my knees had no joints. There was nothing to prevent me from being tossed about. So, I scooched forward, grabbed the metal bar on the seat in front of me, and planted my new Mary Jane shoes firmly on the floor. I stood, legs apart for balance, leaning my back against the seat. Holding tightly to the bar, I prepared for the bus to jerk into gear and propel me forward. I was too distracted by anxiety to look out the window and wave to my mother and brother.

It didn't take long to discover that riding the bus was not the thrill I had imagined. It smelled of grease, bounced up and down like Dad's tractor, and made my stomach queasy.

"Sit up here, silly," Marion instructed, patting the seat. I jumped up and grabbed the edge, but as soon as I settled, we reached the bottom of the hill, arriving at our destination. To that point, Palermo Elementary had been my sister's school. Suddenly I realized I wasn't entirely ready for it to become *my* school. I remember the concerns that overshadowed my excitement about starting school. I worried the teacher wouldn't let me use the restroom when needed. I worried that I wouldn't have any friends. *What if no one wants to sit near me because of the eczema on my hands, arms, and legs? Will they laugh at me? What if I'm not smart enough for kindergarten? How will I know which bus to board when it's time to go home?*

Despite my anxiety, kindergarten was fun, and my teacher, Mrs. McNett, was friendly. Even when correcting one of her students, she used a kind voice. In those days, teachers always wore dresses to school. I remember her plain dresses, usually brown or black. Her dark-rimmed glasses, chunky shoes, and hairnets contributed to my perception that she was old…at least thirty.

Kindergarten introduced me to many exciting activities. I especially enjoyed art and music. A big, inviting easel stood before the row of windows along one side of my classroom. Beside it, generous containers of Tempera paint in brilliant primary colors set on a tray. Each day at center time, I hurried to the easel, determined to possess one of its coveted panels before anyone else. Next to the easel, Mrs. McNett had spread a table with crayons and paper, but they just wouldn't suffice for this budding artist. The experience of drawing with broken or otherwise gnarled crayons could not compare to swirling smooth wet paint across an oversized sheet of clean newsprint.

Because blue was my favorite color, my landscapes started with a massive expanse of azure sky, interrupted by a few cottony clouds. Sometimes I would add a house and a barn, but mostly I painted grassy hills dotted with trees and colorful flowers. I loved mixing primary colors with white or black to create varying green, blue, and pink shades. When I painted, I didn't appreciate being rushed or interrupted. To get the tints and hues just right, I needed time to study the view outside my classroom, where there was a cemetery with an abundance of trees and flowers in the fall and spring and snow-covered tombstones in the winter. I suppose Mrs. McNett thought I was daydreaming because she would remind me to finish up, saying others were waiting for a turn at the easel. Frustration would set in if center time ended before I finished my masterpiece, but I didn't complain. At five years old, I was too timid to express feelings openly.

We gathered on a large oval rag rug near the upright piano during music time. Mrs. McNett played the piano and led us in songs with rhyming words and hand motions. Sometimes she placed large black records on the turntable for lively music to accompany our circle games like "The Farmer in the Dell" or "Ring Around a Rosy." Other times, we tapped the blue Lummi sticks or metal triangles in time with the music.

For me, the best part of music time was the singing. Often Mrs. McNett would call on me to sing a solo. Usually, I felt shy when called upon, trying to melt into the carpet, but not during music time. Singing caused every ounce of self-consciousness to dissipate. Singing made me feel light, free, and confident. At the time, I didn't know music would one day become my career, that I would become a singer, music teacher, and choral conductor. All I knew was that singing brought me joy and much-needed positive attention. It bolstered my fragile self-confidence.

I loved to sing so much that sometimes I sang when I wasn't supposed to. I never would have misbehaved intentionally at school. I would have been mortified to incur the teacher's disapproval. One day during nap time, I began to hum–not a recognizable tune, just some obscure melody from inside my head, where many such themes lived. I didn't realize I had been humming aloud as I rested on my pale-green bath towel. Before long, I sensed a presence hovering above me. I opened my eyes wide enough to spot Mrs. McNett staring downward, hands-on-hips. She was never harsh, but she looked rather imposing at that moment.

"Lucinda," she whispered, using my given name, her tone reminding me of my toddler brother trying to speak quietly in church. "Stop humming. You'll wake the others." Instantly, my face heated with embarrassment, and I was sure I'd be punished. At the age of five, I had no way of knowing that Mrs. McNett's discipline did not consist of shame and blame. Years later, when I became a teacher, I recognized that–whether through instinct or education–Mrs. McNett was committed to giving her young students a positive start in school through gentle training.

As far as I know, my parents never learned of my transgression, nor was there a consequence associated with what I fully expected to be a punishable offense. I continued to love art and music, especially singing, but I never hummed again during kindergarten nap time.

Chapter 7.

A Special Friend

I believe that we should, on biblical grounds, tell all parents of mentally disabled children that God loves their children, regrets terribly that they are disabled, and will, when they die, carry them gently into a heavenly life where every person is forever whole.

~Lewis B. Smedes, Christian author and theology professor

I had a special friend in kindergarten. His name was Wally, but we called him Sonny. I'm not sure why unless it was to distinguish him from Wallace, his father. Sonny's blond hair and blue eyes didn't set him apart. Instead, it was the size of his head. It was much larger than his classmates' heads.

Sonny, who acted less mature than other kindergarteners, liked to sit next to me at the long wooden table and copy everything I did. He was a sweet-natured boy who said funny things, especially when five-year-olds were supposed to be listening instead of talking. I tried not to giggle because I didn't want to get in trouble. I noticed that Mrs. McNett seldom scolded Sonny. She treated him differently from the rest of us. At first, I wondered about it, but I grew to understand that my friend was special.

Maybe I related to Sonny because I, too, was different. At least I felt that way. My extreme allergic eczema and many illnesses kept me home during much of my first school year. In addition to frequent colds, I contracted measles, mumps, strep throat (multiple times), and even hepatitis. Sometimes my eczema was severe enough to keep me from going to school. Often—especially after an illness—Mom would send me to kindergarten wearing white cotton socks on my hands to prevent me from scratching my itchy broken skin. Of course, she was trying to prevent me from catching infectious diseases and missing school. But wearing socks on my hands was embarrassing, causing me to feel like an outcast. I soon learned that Mrs. McNett was in on the conspiracy. Whenever I tried to remove the socks, she made me put them back on.

When I did attend school, Mrs. McNett would ask me to be Sonny's partner

My Kindergarten Friend Sonny

for activities. I liked helping him learn the alphabet by using picture cards and teaching him how to tie his shoes. Helping Sonny made me feel like a teacher. Even in kindergarten, I dreamed of being a teacher. Soon, I discovered Sonny had a good memory—better than mine—and he had become an excellent reader by the end of the year.

Mrs. McNett said I was patient, but I didn't know what "patient" meant. I only knew that I enjoyed being Sonny's friend and showing him how to do things like counting, starting the zipper on his jacket, and mastering wooden puzzles.

The following year, I felt a profound loss when Sonny and I were placed in different classes. Sometimes I'd see him in the lunchroom, and we'd wave at each other from our separate tables.

"Hi, Woo Woo!" He called me Lu Lu, like my mother did at that time. Sonny yelled across the cavernous space, his sandwich flailing in the air. "I gots pea butter 'n jelly today!"

I returned his greeting with a shy wave of my fingers, embarrassed by the outburst directed at me but disappointed we couldn't be together. By the time I reached the second grade, Sonny no longer attended my school. I never saw him again.

A few years ago, I learned of Sonny's death. According to his obituary, he lived to be sixty-five, spending many happy years in a group home. I'm sure God carried him "gently to his heavenly life" where he is "forever whole." I look forward to seeing him again one day.

Chapter 8.

A Secret at Grandma's House

I came from a childhood where I spent a lot of time alone and a lot of time just living with my imagination, and a certain amount of the adult world was kind of alienating.

~Chris Cornell, American musician, singer, and songwriter

When I was three years old, my family moved from my grandparents' home on the dairy farm to a ramshackle house a quarter mile up the road. The yard and the building needed major surgery to turn this property into a home. The house was old, neglected, and lacked indoor plumbing. The barn and chicken coop had long since been abandoned. An overgrown yard blended into the surrounding hayfields, and we soon discovered that snakes lived in the tall grass. Mom, who was determined to create a lawn, spent many hours with a garden hoe, digging up clumps of weeds. That hoe also proved serviceable in beheading snakes.

On moving day, I remember perching on the hay wagon pulled by the team of horses as Dad transported our meager belongings to our "new" house. Marion and I bounced along, seated in the upholstered living room chairs. From that point forward, we referred to our house as "up home," and our grandparents' house became "down home."

One snowy afternoon in 1954, the school bus passed our house, taking

Marion and me "down home." I loved visiting my grandparents' grand old farmhouse with its uneven walls covered in floral wallpaper. Creaky floorboards and wood-burning stoves added to its charm. A picture window, brightening the large country kitchen, framed the barn, silos, and fenced pastures. Another living area and a second kitchen were attached to the house. It was like a duplex, except that both wings shared one bathroom and the second-floor bedrooms. My grandparents still occupied one section, but now the side where my family had lived was inhabited by Uncle Howard (Dad's brother), Aunt Elda, and my cousins, Kathleen and Deanna. Marion and I were glad to have our cousins as playmates, but we weren't happy about the move.

My Grandparents' House
Where I Lived Until I Was 3

To a naïve country girl, Grandma's house seemed huge, stately, and elegantly furnished. Rising from the center foyer was a substantial wooden staircase that led to four bedrooms. My siblings, cousins, and I took pleasure in sliding down the smooth wide banister whenever we thought Grandma wasn't looking. As an adult, I've wondered if she knew of our childish antics and perhaps even welcomed the frequent dustings. Grandma was a fastidious housekeeper who appreciated neatness and the finer things in life. Somehow, she managed to keep the more unpleasant farm odors from permeating her house.

At my paternal grandparents' house, I seldom felt lonely. Maybe it was because my grandmother, a tiny woman of no more than five feet and weighing 100 pounds, while not physically affectionate, talked to me and listened to me respectfully as an equal. She made me feel intelligent, engaging, and above all, cherished.

Grandma was one of the few women of her generation to earn more than a high-school education. At one time, she had been a teacher. To me, she seemed intelligent and sophisticated.

One winter afternoon, Marion and I climbed off the bus and trudged along the snow-covered driveway until we reached the large mudroom that adjoined Grandma's kitchen. After shedding our boots, snow pants, coats, hats, and mittens, we stepped into the house, where I laid my Mighty Mouse lunchbox on the table. My three-year-old brother, Rodger, had just risen from a nap. He walked toward me, sucking his thumb and dragging his tattered blanket with the silky edge. I wrapped an arm around his shoulders, for a moment basking in the identity of "big sister." Quickly Rodger wriggled from my embrace, and I was just me again.

On that snowy Friday afternoon, the grownups had a secret. Grandma greeted us and said we'd eat supper with her and Grandpa and spend the night. I enjoyed staying overnight at their house, but I wondered where my mother was. In those days, children were not given explanations. They were expected to be "seen and not heard."

Marion and I always slept in our favorite bedroom, the large one at the front of the house, with the high ceiling and neatly dressed four-poster bed. The antique furniture and sweet scent of lilacs drew me into its ambiance, filling me with consolation and imagination. I liked to rub my cheek against the smooth lavender-and-white comforter, and I admired how Grandma rolled the pillows in floral bolsters to store them for daytime. She made it look like a luxury hotel room. I would curl up in the big, overstuffed chair that swiveled and rocked to read books or snuggle with my favorite baby doll. The room seemed infused with positive energy, both past and present.

A few years earlier, our frail blind great-grandmother, her long white hair pulled in a tight bun, occupied the room's giant bed day and night. Occasionally, Mom would take Marion and me to visit her. As we stood next to her bed, the tiny, nearly transparent creature would lay a veiny hand on our heads and declare in her trembling voice, "My, how pretty you are, and look how much you've grown!"

That night the room lay uninhabited, ready for two young sisters to luxuriate in its splendor. To us, it was a regal space with its tall elegantly draped windows overlooking a lush, shaded lawn in summer and mammoth snow piles in winter. I felt small but never lonely in this vast welcoming space with its skirted dressing table. The room was a magical place where I could imagine I was a princess, a teacher, or a singer. There I could be anyone I aspired to be.

"Where's Mommy?" I wanted to know when Grandma tucked us in for the night.

"She'll be back tomorrow," answered Grandma. Aware that further questioning would be in vain, Marion and I succumbed to sleep as Grandma closed the door, and a comforting warmth filled the room.

We awakened early to the aroma of sausage drifting up the backstairs from the kitchen below. We called them the backstairs, but they weren't at the rear of the house. Instead, they led to the kitchen through a latched door beside our bed, passing through an attic space. Marion and I talked about exploring the attic filled with storage trunks, old toys, piles of newspapers and magazines, and other fascinating objects. Still, we never asked permission because it was dark and dusty, with spider webs hanging from the rafters. Instead, we slid down the main banister, still dressed in pajamas, and passed through the living and dining rooms. In the kitchen, our grandmother prepared her typical farmer's breakfast of oatmeal or Cream of Wheat with brown sugar and fresh cream, followed by pork sausage, eggs fried in sausage grease, and homemade biscuits slathered with butter and jam.

At 7:00 am, Dad and Grandpa, with red cheeks, came in from the barn where they had finished the morning milking. After depositing their knee-high boots and thick gloves in the mudroom, they removed their fleece-lined coats, coveralls, and silly-looking fur hats with fuzzy earflaps. Taking care not to carry pungent farm odors and debris into the house, they washed their hands at the kitchen sink with Lava soap before sitting, with heavy sighs, at Grandma's feast-laden table.

Earlier, Grandma had added a leaf to the table, extending the length to accommodate my siblings, father, and me. She served the men mugs of hot coffee with cream and sugar. Seated in an antique wooden highchair, Rodger sucked fresh warm milk from a bottle, but Marion and I drank hot Postum, pretending it was coffee. Sipping the delicious grain beverage from Grandma's delicate china teacups made me feel like a grown-up lady. The smooth liquid tasted like the inside of a malt ball and easily slid down my throat, warming my stomach against the chill of a February morning.

In the background, a radio announcer droned on about the expected harsh New York winter as predicted in *The Old Farmer's Almanac*. Next, he advised the best times to plant various crops "come spring." After an advertisement for the local feed 'n' seed store—by "local," he meant eight miles away in Fulton—it was time for *The Arthur Godfrey Show*. I was torn between attending to the radio or listening to Grandpa's entertaining stories about his youth. With his muscular physique from hard physical labor and leathery skin from exposure to the elements, the term "tough old bird" described my grandfather perfectly. His embellished descriptions made farm life sound positively romantic! Dad played along with the anecdotes, but I knew he despised farming. Whenever Grandpa wasn't around, he complained about the hardships characterizing this unchosen occupation into which he had been born.

After breakfast, Grandma announced that Mom and our new baby brother would come home later that day. So, that was the big secret! Later, Marion and I whispered about what it would be like to have a baby in the house. I wondered where babies came from, other than hospitals. My sister, who undoubtedly knew about our mother's pregnancy, had a theory that involved unspeakable vulgarity. I assumed she was concocting another of her elaborate tales to sound clever and grown up. Nevertheless, I was glad it was Saturday, so I didn't have to go to school and miss the exciting event.

Shortly after breakfast, Dad left to pick up Mom and the baby from the hospital in Fulton. I wondered if Mom would let me hold my new brother. I could hardly wait to see him and learn his name. Marion explained that new babies were red and wrinkled with ugly belly buttons. She recalled when Rodger was a newborn, but I was too young to remember since I was only two.

The wait seemed endless. Rodger played with the same ancient metal toy tractors that had entertained our father and uncle as children. As Grandma pumped water into the kitchen sink to wash the breakfast dishes, Rodger ran the tractor back and forth along the wooden floor. He mimicked motor sounds with his mouth, oblivious to the excitement Marion and I shared. She and I parked ourselves by a front window in the dining room, watching and waiting expectantly. Outside, snow fell like goose down, piling high on the driveway and drifting against the front porch railings.

Grandma had a talent for sensing our need for a distraction. Wiping her hands on her ruffled apron, she led us to her first-floor bedroom, where she pulled from under the bed a familiar wooden trunk. Each time she permitted us to open the prized chest that smelled like old books was as thrilling as the first. Grandma had filled it with discarded nightgowns, slips, filmy curtains, and flowing robes of chiffon or satin. We could fashion hours and hours of dramatic play from this cast-off collection. Sometimes we became dignified queens living in far-away exotic lands with scores of attentive servants who obeyed our every command, addressing us as "Your Majesty" or "Your Highness." Other times, we transformed each other—or our cousins—into beautiful brides with extravagant trains trailing behind our curtain-panel veils.

Soon a crunching sound on the driveway's layers of snow and ice interrupted our fantasy. We ran to the kitchen to find Aunt Elda, Aunt Gertrude (Dad's sister) and numerous cousins laden with wrapped gifts and second-hand clothes for the baby. I realized I'd have to share my new brother with many other people.

Finally, Mom arrived, carrying a tiny silent bundle of blue fluff. She looked tired but content. Dad helped her remove her coat and led her to a kitchen chair. My anticipation turned to disappointment when I recognized there was no room for me among the horde of grownups and children surrounding my mother and her swaddled newborn. I heard her say his name was Mark. After Mom handed the sleeping baby to Marion, I tried to climb on her lap for a much needed snuggle, but Rodger had already claimed the spot.

"Not now," Mom said. "Go play with your cousins. Were you a good girl for Grandma?"

"Yes. Can I hold the baby?"

"Later," she answered. "And it's *may* I hold the baby."

Soon, Mom was breastfeeding—or nursing, as it was called then—my new brother and sharing childbirth secrets with the aunts. My cousins and I played games until it was time for them to leave. Dad had already returned to the barn.

"Can I…may I…hold the baby now?"

"He needs a nap, and so do I," my mother said, sighing as she closed the door to Grandma and Grandpa's master bedroom adjacent to the kitchen. Grandma finished cleaning up from breakfast and started peeling potatoes in the sink; Marion worked on a school project at the kitchen table; and Rodger added metal cows and horses to his make-believe farm on the floor.

I left the kitchen, and, passing through the dining room and living room to the foyer, I climbed the stairs. Rounding the upstairs landing, I crossed the threshold to the magical room where reality did not have the power to limit a young girl's imagination.

Chapter 9.

Feeling Without Dealing

Resentment is like taking poison and waiting for the other person to die.

~Attributed to Malachy McCourt and Carrie Fisher, actors

Marion was a tomboy. Rodger and Mark were legitimate boys. Unlike me, they all liked playing outside, working in the barn, and roughhousing. Sometimes in the evening, when Dad was in a good mood, he would wrestle on the floor with my siblings. I might join the tussle to feel included, but I didn't enjoy it. Rolling on the dusty carpet made me wheeze, and I worried I'd get smothered under the pile of bodies. To an asthmatic, the thought of suffocating, unable to draw a breath, seemed the worst possible way to die.

Soon Mom cautioned Dad to "go easy with Lu." I hated it when she protected me like that. It made me feel defective, weak–the family outcast. I desperately needed my father's attention and was sometimes willing to risk an asthma attack to get it. He didn't know how to play with me, and I didn't know how to relate to him. I felt he perceived me as flawed. I tried to be whole, healthy, and carefree, but I was none of those things. I didn't know how to change. I only knew how to be me. Maybe if I were funnier, smarter, sweeter, tougher, kinder, prettier, or perfect, my father would love me.

One night, I told Mom I thought Dad didn't love me. I needed my mother to listen and reassure me. I needed to speak aloud the feelings that had been trapped inside.

She responded as if I had slapped her. "Of course, he loves you! Why would you say such a thing? Do you know how hard your father works to support this family? He's just tired. That's all."

Immediately, I regretted sharing my thoughts.

"Don't tell him," I pleaded. "Please don't tell him what I said."

"Go to sleep," she said, her eyes reflecting injury. "You'll feel better in the morning." How many times had I heard those words? When had I ever felt better in the morning just because the sun rose?

The next evening, Dad was especially attentive to me. He tried to engage me in conversation. When I sat at the piano to practice, he joined me on the bench for the first time and asked questions about my assigned pieces. I should've felt happy. I should've reveled in my father's attention, but all I felt was anger, anger at my mother for betraying my confidence, anger at Mom for putting Dad up to that awkward interaction. Instead of responding to him, I shut him out. The poor man must have been terribly confused.

The next day at naptime, I took a pencil and scribbled circles on my bedroom wall. Big angry circles! First graders shouldn't have to take naps anyway. I regretted my action as soon as I finished, but when I tried to erase the evidence, it smudged and looked worse. I felt ashamed and sorry, but it was too late. The damage was done. When Mom discovered my artwork, she erupted like a volcano, asking questions I couldn't answer. "Why would you do such a thing? What has gotten into you? What's wrong with you?"

How could I tell her I was angry at *her*? No, I couldn't risk alienating my primary caregiver.

Looking more hurt than angry, Mom turned and walked out, leaving me to wonder when the punishment would occur and what the consequence would be. I waited, but she didn't return. Eventually, I emerged from my room, but the incident was never mentioned again.

Since we never discussed the issue, we never resolved it. My father and I continued to struggle with our awkward relationship, and I seldom felt comfortable sharing honest feelings with my mother. Neither of these practices proved mentally or emotionally healthy.

Chapter 10.

Wash Day

I don't remember my mother ever playing with me. And she was a perfectly good mother. But she had to do the laundry and clean the house and do the grocery shopping.

~Patricia Heaton, American actress

Wash day on the farm was just that—an entire day devoted to washing clothes. During the week, the electric wringer machine stood against a kitchen wall. Above it was a shelf that held our home's only radio. Many evenings my siblings and I would climb inside the washer's metal tub with our favorite blankets and listen to classic radio programs like *The Adventures of Rin Tin Tin*, *The Lone Ranger*, and *The Jack Benny Program*.

When Saturday morning rolled around, so did the wringer washer. Mom moved it to the white kitchen sink with its built-in drainboard. The task started early and lasted until suppertime. After Mom gathered a week's worth of dirty clothes, including diapers, from her family of six, she divided them into piles on the kitchen floor. Next, she hauled buckets of clear water from the well in the front yard. Even after our house had indoor plumbing, she couldn't use the running water for laundry because it was filled with rust that stained everything red.

Washing clothes was serious business, allowing no time for mischief. Our mother wasn't amused when Rodger and I made a game of jumping in the mounds of clothes, scattering them like leaves in an autumn wind. With hands-on-hips, she would sigh and yell in frustration, "Scram, you two! Go outside and run around!"

Filling the tub with bucket after bucket of water heated on the kitchen stove, Mom began with the "whites," tossing them into the machine and adding a scoop of Fab detergent. Colgate no longer manufactures Fab, but I'll never forget its intense aromatic scent.

During the wash cycle, our mother scurried about accomplishing other household tasks. As soon as each load finished, she lifted the wet, soapy clothes into the sink for rinsing in clear cold water, then fed them piece-by-piece through the wringer to squeeze out the excess. The wringer was most effective in that regard. Mom's mending pile always included a few cracked buttons that she would need to replace at the end of the month.

Into the tub went more loads, each darker in color and more soiled. While Mom changed the rinse water every time, she reused the wash water repeatedly, saving Dad's farm-filthy overalls for last. With the rinse cycle finished, she scooped up the damp clothes from the drainboard and tossed them into a wicker laundry basket. Each holding a handle, Marion and I would haul the heavy baskets, one at a time, to the backyard, where long clotheslines stretched between two sturdy tee-shaped poles.

Our household chores evolved as we grew. As soon as my sister and I were tall enough, our job was to shake and pin the clothes to the lines. Mom showed us how to conserve clothespins by overlapping the edges of multiple items. Why she couldn't purchase a second set of pins, we didn't understand at the time, but I surmise it had to do with growing up during the Great Depression.

We didn't mind the job so much in the summer because it afforded us a welcome opportunity to soak up some rare sunshine and enjoy the pleasant breezes that characterized New York's summers. To this day, I can think of no sweeter smell than the scent of freshly laundered sheets that have dried in the sun.

In the winter, Mom had to remove the clotheslines to prevent them from being buried under snowbanks that piled taller and taller each time Dad cleared the rear driveway with a snowplow affixed to his tractor. During inclement weather, we lugged the baskets upstairs to the wide hallway strung with multiple lines that sagged as we added soggy dungarees (as we called blue jeans), towels, tee-shirts, and underwear.

An exposed metal pipe, about a foot in circumference, ran from the wood furnace in the cellar through the first-floor dining room, then upstairs where it attached to the chimney. We didn't have to touch the hot metal more than once to learn of its danger. The heat it generated caused the wet laundry to dry quickly.

As soon as the clothes dried, Marion and I removed and folded them, making space for the next load.

When, at last, we had completed the mammoth task, Mom drained the washing machine of its grimy gray water. Then, she wiped the tub dry and rolled the washer to its resting place against the kitchen wall, where it would remain until the following Saturday.

A Typical Winter View of Our House from the Backyard

Chapter 11.

A Painful Lesson

Anger ventilated often hurries toward forgiveness and concealed often hardens into revenge.

~Edward G. Bulwer-Lytton, 19th-century English writer and politician

I was afraid of most animals on the farm, including dogs, but especially rodents. I could hear mice scratching in the space between the old farmhouse walls at night. I was terrified they would get into my bedroom, crawl on me, and maybe even nibble my toes. Sometimes I dreamed about being devoured by hundreds of mice with beady eyes and sharp teeth. I would tuck the blanket snugly around my legs and pull the covers over my head as if that could prevent their entrance into my safe sanctuary.

Birds were the only creatures that didn't elicit fear or make me sneeze or itch. One summer day, I discovered two baby robins beneath a maple tree. I knew they were robins because I had seen their mother sitting in the nest and their red-breasted father flitting nearby. These babies were far from mature enough to enter flight school, and their nest was too high for me to reinstate them. Perhaps they had tried to fly or were kicked out by their mother. I wondered how they had survived the fall. Whatever the circumstance, I was determined to rescue them. As I scooped them up gently, their yellow-rimmed beaks opened wide, begging to be filled. I ran inside and up the stairs to place the helpless creatures in an empty shoebox. Instinctively, I knew they needed warmth. Remembering the heat produced by my desk lamp, I set the rectangular nursery under it and switched it on. Again, the frail infants begged mutely for food. I ran downstairs to the kitchen where Mom was working at the sink.

"What do birds eat?" I asked.

Accustomed to her daughter's frequent questions, Mom answered without looking away from her preparations, "Well, some birds eat seeds and berries, and others eat worms."

"What about baby robins?" I asked.

"The mommy robins eat worms and then regurgitate them into the babies' mouths."

"What's regurgitate?" I wanted to know. Mom, who was uncomfortable with graphic language, thought carefully before answering.

"Um, she swallows the food to make it soft and easy for the babies to digest. Then she feeds it to them." I had to visualize the process before I realized what she meant.

"Ugh! You mean she throws up?"

"Well, um, yes," Mom answered. I tried to imagine chewing a worm, swallowing it, and then vomiting on purpose...the thought caused me to nearly lose my own breakfast.

"What if the babies have fallen out of the nest?" I asked.

"They don't usually survive. Why do you ask?"

"I found some baby birds on the ground."

"Where are they now?"

"In my room. What should I feed them?"

"They probably won't make it. Are you keeping them warm?"

"Yes, they're under my lamp. Come and see."

"I have to finish snapping the beans. I'll come in a few minutes."

I returned to my room to keep vigil over the babies huddled together in the corner of the shoebox. They didn't have feathers yet. Instead, wispy gray fuzz covered their tiny forms. I decided to name them Angel and Sunshine. When they were strong enough, I'd return them to the wild. I imagined Angel and Sunshine coming back to me every spring. Of course, I'd recognize them just as any mother would know her own.

Soon Mom appeared in the doorway carrying a bowl of bread soaked in milk and a medicine dropper. "Here. Try this," she suggested. "Start slowly with just a drop or two. Now don't get too attached. They probably won't live through the night." I was determined not to let Mom's pragmatism burst my bubbles of hope.

I set my alarm clock to wake me at 2:00 am each morning. Groggily, I got up and administered the doughy substance, hoping to sustain life and promote growth. Two days later, my helpless charges seemed to be thriving. Soon a fluffy down covered their transparent skin, and they cheeped at me as if they recognized me. Now they were ready to graduate to worms, I decided.

The following day after breakfast, I headed for the garden with a trowel. I dug in the dirt for earthworms, which were plentiful after an early morning rain shower. I mashed them with the scoop and fed them to my adopted babies. It gave me a sense of purpose and genuine accomplishment for the first time in my young life. Two living creatures depended on me for their existence, and I had kept them alive, thriving even.

A few days later, I noticed the first feathers. Angel and Sunshine now flapped their wings, practicing for a future flight. The once tiny, huddled mass of beaks and fuzz gradually transformed into two distinct creatures who squawked at me whenever I passed their cardboard bassinet. I felt a sense of purpose as they showed signs of developing into healthy birds. I dreamed of teaching them how to unearth worms for themselves and how to fly. It would be painful to watch them strike out on their own, but, simultaneously, I would feel exhilarated by my achievement as a surrogate parent.

Minutes later, I climbed the back-porch steps, carrying my daily ration of baby-robin-feast in a tin can, noticing someone had left the back door ajar. As I entered the kitchen, I spotted one of the farm cats descending the stairs. It was carrying something in its mouth. No, it couldn't be! But it was. I bolted up the stairs, my heart racing. Finding an empty shoebox, I flew down the stairs in a rage. I was so angry and upset that my reaction frightened me, but I couldn't stop screaming and crying. Mom grabbed me and pulled me to her apron, declaring, "Oh, honey, I'm sorry!"

For a moment, I felt comforted, but my grief was inconsolable, my anger beyond control. "Stupid cat! I hate that stupid cat!" screamed a voice I didn't recognize.

"Don't say hate. It's not the cat's fault," retorted Mom, now pushing me away, suddenly transformed from comforter to scolder. My mother wasn't comfortable with strong words or negative emotions and often tried to talk me out of mine. I turned my face into a corner, buried it in my hands, and kicked the wall, my anger and disappointment too strong for a young girl to handle.

"Hate, hate, hate!" I shrieked as hot tears streamed down my cheeks. I couldn't stop the explosion. It felt like I was possessed by something outside myself. "How could God let it happen? I hate God!" That's when Mom grabbed my shoulders, turned me toward her, and shook me. In that moment, she didn't understand that one stage of grief—probably the first stage—was anger. She was too shocked by my outburst to comprehend that children's words don't have filters, especially when they are upset.

"Don't ever say that again, young lady!" Even as I had said it, I knew I was pushing the envelope of my mother's sympathy, but I couldn't stop myself. I was crushed by sadness and disappointment. Of course, I didn't hate God, but uttering such intense words was the most extreme reaction I could muster, and this tragedy called for an extreme response.

I ran up the stairs to my room, slammed the door, threw myself on my bed, and sobbed, both grief and guilt washing over me in powerful waves.

Later, as I emptied the shoebox that had failed to protect my tiny charges, I wished I could return to the moment of my mother's comforting hug, but it was too late.

I would recover from my loss. Children are resilient, after all. But the experience shaped a subconscious determination that I would never again allow myself to become attached to an animal.

Chapter 12.

The State Fair

If you ever start feeling like you have the goofiest, craziest, most dysfunctional family in the world, all you have to do is go to a state fair. Because five minutes at the fair, you'll be going, 'You know, we're alright. We're dang near royalty'.

~Jeff Foxworthy, American comedian

I was young when I discovered that farmers didn't get vacations. Therefore, farmers' families didn't get vacations, either. The vocation of my father and grandfather was demanding and relentless, with no one to relieve them for more than a day if they wanted to take time off. As Dad often remarked, "The cows won't milk themselves."

From my earliest memory, my family eagerly anticipated the one day of the year when Dad could leave the cows and crops behind and drive us some twenty-five miles to the New York State Fair near Syracuse. For that one auspicious day, Grandpa would hire a farmhand to shoulder Dad's chores, so we could take our annual holiday. Because it was so seldom that we went anywhere special, when we did, it was an occasion for dressing up and looking our best. No farmer's dungarees would do for the fair.

Mom's preparations began several days before the event, ensuring that as soon as Dad and Grandpa finished the morning milking, our family of six could pile into our navy-blue Nash Ambassador. Mom loaded the spacious trunk with enough food and drinks to feed her family of six for the day. She made everything "from scratch" even after the invention of cake mixes and sliced deli meats. Homemade bread and hand-churned butter came from her kitchen, also delicious cookies, fresh-squeezed lemonade, baked ham or roast beef for sandwiches, and fresh or home-canned vegetables from the garden. For our day at the fair, she packed the perishables in cardboard boxes, surrounding them with large chunks of ice and layers of newspaper to prevent spoilage in the hot summer sun.

The fairground was only twenty-five miles away, but the trip seemed to take forever. Filled with excitement, we grew restless. We squabbled and wrestled in the backseat until Dad threatened to turn the car around. Of course, we knew his threat was empty because he wanted to go as much as we did. It was then that Mom usually got us singing. Soon we were belting out songs like "You are My Sunshine" and "I've Been Workin' on the Railroad," with Marion singing alto and me adding a descant while Mom helped our brothers with the melody.

Entrance to the New York State Fair

At last, Dad found a parking space in the large gravel lot surrounding the fairground and bought our tickets. As soon as we passed through the gate, I could smell the popcorn and hear distant calliope music emanating from the midway. The place was swarming with people of all ages. They seemed to know exactly where they were going and were hurrying to get there. When their paths intersected with mine, I would have to release Mom's hand and jump out of the way.

As soon as Dad considered my brothers old enough, he allowed them to accompany him to the 4-H barns, where judges handed out ribbons for cows, pigs, and goats based on criteria that eluded me. Next, they would visit the farm-implement displays with plans to meet us at noon for a picnic lunch.

My sister and I accompanied Mom to a long building where we walked along the center aisle admiring row-upon-row of prize-winning quilts in interesting colors and designs. No temporary tents graced this fairground. Its solid concrete walls and floors were built to endure for generations, and they have. In the next building, we viewed hundreds of vases of exquisitely arranged flowers: zinnias, dahlias, marigolds, and lilies. Their colorful petals seemed to dance among copious green fronds.

Beyond that building, we found displays of pies in every flavor from mince to blueberry, plus miles of homemade jams, jellies, and crafts of every sort, expertly fashioned from organic materials. We walked up one aisle and down another until my short legs begged to rest. But we hadn't finished yet. A whole structure filled with award-winning fruits and vegetables awaited us. Now I was not only tired but hungry and thirsty, too. Being surrounded by food didn't help me cope. For some reason, I always failed to remember this tedious, exhausting aspect of the fair when time came for the next year's event.

Because the cost of fairground food was prohibitive for farm families—at least that's what our parents told us—we returned to the car for a picnic lunch of cold fried chicken or roast beef sandwiches. The feast usually included Mom's famous macaroni or potato salad and fresh-squeezed lemonade mixed with orange juice. She might even top off our feast with gooey Toll House cookies, another of her specialties. With full stomachs and excitement coursing through our bodies, we approached the midway to soak in its flashing lights and irresistible sounds of children squealing, barkers barking, riders screaming, and vendors hawking their wares. All this stimulation mixed with festive music from many sources overwhelmed my senses. I could cope only because I knew it was time for our one ride on the Ferris wheel.

Waiting in line with my coveted ticket, I feared I might wet my pants as I anticipated soaring high above the fairground. Despite butterflies hijacking my lunch, I could observe the crowds of bustling fairgoers below for a few precious moments. My brothers would have preferred the thrill of spinning on octopus' arms or traversing the roller coaster's steep ups and downs. But the Ferris wheel's leisurely revolutions afforded me more than enough excitement.

As soon as the ride ended, we begged to go again, but Dad always insisted it was a waste of money. "Once is enough," he would say. Of course, we wanted to return to the midway to play games and win Teddy bears, but that, too, was out of the question on a farmer's income. As much as the irresistible smell of cotton candy, popcorn, and funnel cake lured us, we knew such treats were for other children, not us.

Instead, we spent the afternoon at the horse pavilion watching Western and English equestrian events. It was my sister's favorite part of the fair, and I learned not to disturb her while she happily endured the hot sun and unpleasant odors. As still as a bird mesmerized by an earthworm in the ground, she sat with wide eyes riveted on the show ring. Marion had always wanted a horse of her own to ride and care for, but I was afraid of horses and allergic to them. The workhorses on our farm were huge and scary. I couldn't imagine climbing high enough to sit on one or attempting to control the mammoth beast. Furthermore, just walking past their stalls precipitated fits of sneezing, wheezing, and runny eyes.

For me, evenings at the fair were magical. While Dad retrieved our supper picnic from the car, Mom scouted out a prime spot in front of the bandstand. Then, Dad spread a large army-green blanket on the ground. We crunched fresh fruits and vegetables from our reverently tended garden and feasted on Mom's delicious, homemade bread and butter. No French fries, sodas, or cotton candy for us. At the time, I thought we were deprived, but today, I'd give anything to taste Mom's home-baked bread again.

As the hot August sun approached the horizon, sparkling lights and fireflies turned the fairground into a fairyland, and dusk ushered in a soothing breeze typical of summer evenings in New York. Twilight, when our family settled in for an evening of world-class entertainment, was the best time at the fair. This was what I had waited for all day. Even the Ferris wheel ride couldn't compare. Among other well-known stars of the day, we enjoyed the likes of the Lennon Sisters and Ray Charles. Another year, Gene Autry and his band performed. He even brought his clever horse, Champion, who did tricks for an appreciative audience, especially my would-be cowboy brothers.

Eventually, the boys would fall asleep, but Marion and I sat spellbound by the fantastic spectacle of sight and sound. It was a singular treat to be entertained by famous performers we had seen only on our black-and-white television. Every year, I resolved that I would be singing on that stage one day. I would have a trunk full of extravagant sequined costumes and tour the country in a fancy bus with my name brandished across each side.

As I sat cross-legged and wide-eyed, mesmerized by stimuli too vivid to absorb at once, I imagined my future performing career. The New York State Fair was where a young girl's dreams could soar unfettered for one glorious day each year.

Chapter 13.

The Fire

I love those who can smile in trouble, who can gather strength from distress, and grow brave by reflection...

~Leonardo da Vinci

It happened in the early hours of a cold winter morning when I was seven. I shared the big iron bed on the second floor of our old farmhouse with my sister, who was nine. It was still dark outside when we awakened to the faint smell of smoke and heard sirens blaring. Downstairs, Mom was talking on the phone in a concerned tone, but I couldn't make out her muffled words. Marion and I pulled the covers over our heads and whispered until Mom appeared at our bedroom door.

"Get up and dress quickly," she said.

"What's going on?" Marion asked.

"I'll tell you after you've dressed," Mom called as she hurried back down the stairs. "Wear something warm." We rushed to the window. Gazing beyond the barn, we saw smoke ascending from the town center. Palermo, New York, where I lived until I was eighteen, wasn't a town. Instead, numerous dairy farms like ours converged at an intersection where a few non-farmhouses surrounded our elementary school.

"Somebody's house is on fire," Marion said. In the distance, we could see flashing red lights piercing the darkness, and it seemed there were more cars than usual headed in that direction along County Route 45.

After pulling on our clothes from the day before, we rushed downstairs to find Mom brewing vats of coffee on the large wood-burning stove that dominated our kitchen.

"What's going on?" Marion asked. "I hear sirens."

Without answering, Mom issued a series of orders in an unusual tone, indicating that arguing would not be tolerated. "Girls, eat quickly. Then help your brothers with their snowsuits...and hurry."

"What's happening?" I asked. "Is somebody's house on fire?"

"I'll tell you on the way. Just hurry," Mom repeated. She wiped Mark's face and hands with a wet dishrag, pulled him out of the highchair, and handed him to me.

"On the way where?" Still no answer. Mom was busily pouring steaming coffee into large thermoses before donning her snow boots and heavy wool coat with the faux fur collar.

With everyone dressed, Mom ushered us out the back door, where we trudged through new-fallen snow and walked as briskly as our short legs could carry us down the hill toward the clouds of black smoke. Marion carried Mark piggyback, and I held Rodger's hand as Mom pulled his red wagon loaded with containers of cream and sugar, stacks of cardboard coffee cups, and thermoses that sloshed as we walked. By eight o'clock, we arrived at the scene to find our entire little community gathered in the gravel parking lot of our elementary school. A sheriff directed us to stand near the school bus garage on the opposite side of the driveway, where we'd be a safe distance from the blaze and the black cloud rising from our school. For a moment, the thick smoke filled our nostrils.

Original Palermo Elementary School, a Winter Entryway Covering the Arched Front Door

Mom set the thermoses on the ground and lifted two-year-old Mark into the wagon. As Marion shook her arms and sighed with relief, Mom instructed us to stand under a bare maple tree beside the bus garage and keep an eye on our brothers. We were bundled in snowsuits, boots, hats, and mittens to defend against the chill, and our breathing created puffs of vapor as it hit the frigid morning air. I grabbed Marion's coat sleeve and stood close to her, frightened and confused by all the commotion.

On the way, Mom had tried to prepare us by explaining that there was a fire at the school, but seeing our beloved school building engulfed in flames was shocking. As she approached a group of other young mothers, her eyes darted back and forth from her children to the blaze. The women pointed and waved their arms, but I couldn't hear their words amid all the ruckus. Still holding Rodger's hand, I buried my face in Marion's coat, anxious to see what was happening but afraid to look.

Then, daring to peek, I spotted the inside of my wallless second-grade classroom, where snow and ashes fell on my wooden desk. Then, with a gasp, I watched the remaining walls crumble. I remembered my Tinkerbell pencil case and the new box of crayons I had acquired only days before. I looked for my colorful flower painting that Mrs. Rowe had hung on the wall above my cubby. It was gone. The cubby where I hung my coat and stored my boots and lunchbox each day was gone. Scanning the unrecognizable building, I searched for my favorite room, the library. It, too, was razed. Suddenly, the school's front entrance collapsed, reduced to wet black smoldering ruins. At first, I tried to be brave, but once I saw some of the adults crying, I let my tears flow.

A heavy cloud hung in the piercing winter air. The smell reminded me of whenever Dad opened the cellar furnace to add huge chunks of firewood. The house would fill with smoke, choking us for a few minutes. But this smoke was different. Angry and black, its haze was menacing.

We watched the firefighters rushing about with hoses from a tanker truck, yelling instructions. We knew they could do nothing more to stop the destruction. Helplessness replaced the initial adrenalin rush of Mom's urgency.

Bits and pieces of the adults' conversations mentioned arson. I didn't know what that word meant until I overheard a neighbor claiming to have seen two men wearing ski masks climbing out the cafeteria window just before dawn. She said they disappeared through the cemetery next to the school's property. To this day, I don't know if the culprits were ever caught.

Until that morning, I took my school for granted. I rose each morning, dressed, ate breakfast, and boarded the bus. In my childish perception, the routine would continue without interruption. I never imagined the beautiful brick building that welcomed me through its arched doorway each morning might one day cease to exist.

Mark was too young to understand anything other than the excitement of fire trucks and police cars with sirens screaming and lights flashing. Unlike his school-aged siblings, he wouldn't be altered by the incident or "grow brave by reflection" of its memory.

Rodger stood mute, staring through giant orbs that reflected red spinning lights. His long eyelashes grabbed and held snowflakes as they drifted from a gray sky.

Often, it takes an unsuspecting child to provide much-needed comic relief during anxious moments. Five-year-old Rodger looked up at Mom with wide-eyed innocence and proclaimed, "But I didn't even get to finish kindergarten!" I suppose, to him, the fire marked the end of his academic career. I could tell that the adults' spontaneous laughter startled and confused him. He was too young to understand that sometimes adults laugh amid distress to keep from falling apart.

Finally, with the thick veil of tension broken, dozens of onlookers sprang into action, trying to help the firefighters win their losing battle. With yellow suits pulled over their usual dungarees, volunteer firefighters moved to each new blazing section, flooding it with water from fat hoses and narrowly escaping the caving walls. Other helpers rushed in, trying to salvage a few desks, chairs, and books from the smoldering rubble, but their mission was hopeless.

Soon Dad arrived from his early morning chores. My brothers started to rush toward the comfort of his strong arms, but Mom pushed them back to our place of safety, and Dad joined the efforts to extinguish any remaining flames.

Once the fire was under control and the building flattened to rubble, Mom and the other women served coffee and donuts to the weary firefighters. I suppose it made them feel useful. Despite the grave situation, there was a sense of community spirit—a coming together—that felt solid and comforting, like when families gather for the funeral of a loved one and table any resentments for the day.

Re-built Palermo School

For the remainder of the school year, my siblings and I endured a bumpy, eight-mile bus ride to the town of Mexico, New York, where some students gathered in houses and churches. My class met in the industrial arts room in the high school's basement, and Rodger got to finish kindergarten.

By the time Mark started kindergarten three years later, we had a new elementary school. This shiny steel-beamed sterile structure stretched longer and broader and included a sprinkler system. Although the new building was safe, cost-effective, and modern in design, it lacked its predecessor's warmth, history, and charm.

Chapter 14.

Inauspicious Ancestors

To forget one's ancestors is to be a brook without a source, a tree without a root.

~Chinese Proverb

In researching their genealogy, many families discover they have famous or accomplished ancestors about whom they can boast. Our family's claim to fame—or shame—was the less-than-stellar Loomis Gang, an outlaw family of horse thieves under the patriarchy of George Washington Loomis (1779-1851). Although the gang's criminal behavior in Central New York happened in the 19th century, I heard many legends about it from Grandpa Loomis, Dad's father. Members of the infamous Loomis family (G.W. Loomis' children) were still living when my grandfather was born in 1891, making him only a generation removed from the height of the Loomis Gang's terrorization of Central New York and beyond.

I remember Grandpa's animated stories about the Loomis Gang. I wondered why he seemed proud to be related to violent outlaws who managed to escape justice. Grandpa kept a book entitled *The Loomis Gang* by George W. Walter on his bookshelf in the living room, but I never felt the need to open it. It was embarrassing to discover I might be related to hardened criminals; however intelligent and clever Grandpa made them seem. Although Grandpa's enthusiasm came across as pride, he may have simply found the stories of the Loomis Gang's escapades fascinating.

When I was young, I feared someone at school would discover my lineage and tease me about it. Fortunately, our New York State history study in the fourth grade did not include the Loomis Gang.

I decided to do some research since a Loomis memoir wouldn't be complete without mentioning the notorious gang. Because there are few reliable sources about my inauspicious ancestors, I wondered why history books didn't say anything about the largest family outlaw gang in the United States at the time. That is until I focused on what else was happening in our country then.

National events of the mid-1800s included John Brown's abolitionist efforts and subsequent martyrdom. Abraham Lincoln was elected President of the United States in 1860, and the US Civil War broke out in 1861. After General Lee surrendered in 1865, Lincoln was re-elected, only to be assassinated a few days later. As a result of the war, slavery was abolished, and the first meeting of the Ku Klux Klan took place. In 1869, Elizabeth Cady Stanton and Susan B. Anthony created the National Woman Suffrage Association, which eventually won the right for women to vote. During the Loomis Gang's heyday, the country was embroiled in such monumental events that all but the citizens of Central New York were distracted from the gang's illicit affairs. The gang members made sure they profited from every event.

I wanted to know if my ancestors had always been criminals. I learned that Joseph Loomis, the original immigrant who arrived from England in the early seventeenth century, was a well-respected man. The Loomises who settled in New England were wealthy, educated, and refined. So, what happened?

It seems the family turned to its criminal ways a century later after one

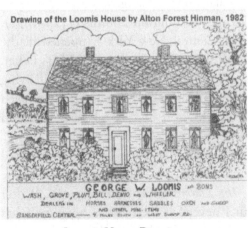

Drawing of the Loomis House by Alton Forest Hinman, 1982

Loomis House Drawing

of Joseph's successors, George Washington Loomis (1823-1865), married Rhoda Mallet, the daughter of an officer in the French Revolution Army. George and Rhoda purchased land near Nine Mile Point in Sangerfield, New York. Both had been members of New England's aristocracy and had plenty of money to buy land and live in luxury. They built a house, barn, and later a larger home to accommodate their growing family on a hill overlooking Nine Mile Swamp. This mansion was big enough to house their offspring while concealing numerous non-family members of the gang from the law. Included in the construction were many hiding places for stolen goods. It soon became the syndicate's headquarters. Since their second house was built on a high summit, they could spot men approaching on horseback from miles away.

Although the farm that raised cattle and sheep and grew hops became

successful, its profits weren't enough to satisfy Rhoda, who instructed her children to participate in petty thefts. Eventually, George and Rhoda had twelve children, ten of whom lived to adulthood. Soon, their shoplifting led them to more serious criminal activity. Rhoda taught her children that stealing was okay if they didn't get caught.

Brian Falk, a journalist native of nearby Waterville, stated in his documentary, "The Loomis Gang," that the Loomis children, unlike most criminals, were "intelligent, sophisticated, and well-educated." Rhoda, who supported the idea of female equality, ensured that even her girls received opportunities to study. In addition to their education, the girls progressed quickly from

Rhoda "Ma" Loomis

petty theft to shoplifting, then home invasions and counterfeiting, and they even helped their brothers stage highway robberies. But the Loomis men specialized in stealing horses. Falk states they would hide stolen animals in the nearby Nine Mile Swamp, change their markings with bleach and potato dye, and sell them. Sometimes they even sold them back to the original owners!

As my research continued, I began comparing what I was learning about the Loomis Gang with what I knew about my Loomis family, especially my father and grandfather, who were direct descendants, according to Grandpa. Despite Grandpa's local reputation as a shrewd horse- and cow-trader, I knew him to be honest, law-

Lucia Loomis, Rhoda's Daughter

abiding, and hardworking. As farmers, my father and grandfather survived the Great Depression, endless harsh winters, a tornado that tore the roof off the dairy barn, and two fires that burned it to the ground. Twice they had to rebuild from the ground up. I'm sure each of those stressful events could tempt any honest man. Yet, they did not turn to crime.

Loomis Gang Wanted Poster

I became curious about what motivated the Loomis Gang's criminal behavior, especially since money was not scarce. Was stealing merely a recreational pastime for the spoiled and entitled Loomis kids? Which generation, I wondered, broke the cycle and changed the direction of my ancestors' lives?

Dr. E. Fuller Torrey, a native of Clinton, New York, evidently shared my curiosity. In 1992, after extensive research, he published *Frontier Justice: The Rise and Fall of the Loomis Gang*, the most comprehensive book I've found on the subject. Until then, George Walter's book—the one I remember seeing on my grandfather's bookshelf—was the only published account of a ruthless crime syndicate terrorizing the eastern United States during the nineteenth century.

According to Torrey, when George Washington Loomis Senior died in 1852, the Loomis Gang's leadership skipped his feeble-minded eldest son. It fell to his second son, George Washington Loomis Junior, known as Wash. Apparently, Wash was charming, intelligent, and handsome, but he was also ruthless.

Wash and his younger brother, Grove, expanded the business of horse theft by subcontracting to non-family members. This practice increased profits while making it harder for law officials to trace the crimes back to them. As Wash and Grove continued to build their organization, adding more than two hundred non-family agents, the syndicate spread west to the Finger Lakes, north to Canada, east to Vermont and Connecticut, and south to Virginia.

But their mother, Rhoda, controlled all her children, holding the family together and not in a loving maternal way. I remember Grandpa Loomis referring to "Ma Loomis" (Rhoda) as the true leader of the gang. According to Torrey, Rhoda felt superior to her neighbors because of her aristocratic background and considered her children entitled to whatever they could steal.

Armed with money and charm, Wash Loomis quickly bought the protection of local law enforcement and frequently bribed the legislators in Albany. From apprenticing with lawyers in Waterville during his youth, Wash knew about the legal system, and since many local officials were dishonest, he was able to buy their protection from prosecution. In addition to bribery, Wash, Grove, and Wheeler used violence, including burning property and destroying evidence against them. They even set fire to the Sangerfield Courthouse to destroy indictments against them and delay court proceedings. As the gang ravaged the Waterville and Sangerfield communities, fear of robbery and reprisals grew among their citizens.

George Washington Loomis, Jr.

"Wash"

Wash Loomis

When the Civil War broke out, it provided the gang with another profitable business: selling stolen horses to the Union Army. While the Loomis men avoided serving in the army, they stayed busy stealing the same horses back and selling them again to other units. Soon, a second opportunity presented itself. The gang sent members to enlist, collect the fifteen-dollar recruitment fee, and then desert and enroll elsewhere.

During the war, Jim Filkins managed to get himself elected sheriff of Waterville. Determined to stop the gang's reign of terror, he increased arrests and indictments against Wash, Grove, Wheeler, and their younger brothers, Plumb and Denio. But the Loomis men retaliated violently, shooting into Filkins' house, missing his wife and children but wounding him.

This is when internal feuds began to divide the Loomis family. Wash and Grove wanted to expand the network, while Plumb and Denio sided with greedy Rhoda, who preferred to limit the gang's size to avoid sharing the spoils. After authorities charged Wheeler with rape, he fled to Canada.

In 1865, a vigilante group formed in Waterville, but they couldn't outsmart the

Grove Loomis

Loomises, who had connections in high places. A constant menace in Waterville and the surrounding towns, the Gang seemed invincible.

When the war veterans returned to Central New York, they were irate to find the Loomis men had avoided military service. The family still controlled Waterville and Sangerfield, slipping through prosecution with threats, bribery, and violence. The veterans joined Filkins in secret meetings to form a citizens' vigilante group. Its purpose was to get rid of the Loomis Gang at last. At that time in America's history, it was common for citizens to take the law into their own hands. A Wild West atmosphere was widespread even in the Eastern states, and violence seemed the only way to break the Loomis Gang's powerful control.

Filkins began leading nighttime raids on the Loomis mansion, which was well-protected by lookouts during the day. The attacks resulted in gunfights, multiple arrests, and daring escapes. But the Loomises always avoided prosecution.

After recovering from wounds inflicted in the attack on his house, Filkins again led a midnight raid on the Loomis farm, this time with the intention of killing them. He provoked Wash to flee from the house, where he took him out back and beat him to death. He also set fire to the Loomis barn and attempted to burn Grove alive. Filkins was prosecuted for murder, but the townspeople of Waterville and nearby Brookfield rejoiced at the news of Wash's death, hopeful the gang would fall apart without him. After his release on bail, a determined Filkins returned, formed another posse, and stormed the property again, first poisoning the Loomis' guard dogs, then entering the house with guns drawn. The Loomises wounded him a second time.

A week later, another group of about a hundred vigilantes surrounded the Loomis homestead and stormed the house. As some started lynching Plumb Loomis, others set fire to the house, causing Rhoda and her daughters to flee to the yard. The women tried to save their belongings as their attackers threw their possessions back into the burning house faster than they could retrieve them. The group raised Plumb to a sturdy branch three times but, in the end, spared his life by convincing him to name other gang members. This act left the once-wealthy Loomis family financially ruined and began the gang's collapse.

Because of area-wide hatred toward the Loomis Gang, the Supreme Court overturned Jim Filkins' indictment despite overwhelming evidence that he had murdered Wash. The gang disbanded, and while individual crimes continued, many remaining members left. Even Rhoda, now destitute, lived quietly to the age of ninety-four.

It was not easy to unearth a comprehensive history of the Loomis Gang. It's likely that many of my fellow Loomis descendants and their communities have worked to play down their ancestors' infamy. Indeed, being related to violent criminals is not a reason for pride, but we can't change history.

I tried unsuccessfully to track my ancestry, hoping to link my grandfather to Joseph, the original immigrant from England. I would like to think my lineage traces to him or Bill Loomis, the only son who escaped Rhoda's evil influence, but I guess I'll never know. I know that my father and grandfather were pillars of their small community of Palermo, New York. I know that Dad's brother, Howard, served his country honorably in WWII, their cousin, Wendall, was a respected veterinarian, and most of the Loomises in my life were honest, hardworking farmers.

Now that I have more information about my Loomis ancestors than my grandfather did, I am compelled to agree with him. The history of the Loomis Gang, though terrible, is fascinating.

I learned that a few years ago, Waterville, New York's Historical Society, found a way to cash in on the Loomis Gang's local notoriety. As part of its Summer Festival in August, it offers a Loomis Gang Country Bus Tour, which sells out. The society even sets up a unique Loomis Store where one can purchase such items as postcards, mugs, books, and even a Wash Loomis tee shirt.

I must add the Waterville Summer Festival to my bucket list. But they can keep the tee shirt.

Bibliography:

Falk, Brian, "The Loomis Gang," a documentary released in 2002

Torrey, E. Fuller, *Frontier Justice: The Rise and Fall of the Loomis Gang*, North Country Books, Inc. 1992

Walter, George W, *The Loomis Gang*, Prospect Books, 1953

Chapter 15.

Music and Church

The Church knew what the psalmist knew: Music praises God. Music is well or better able to praise him than the building of the church and all its decoration; it is the Church's greatest ornament.

~Igor Stravinsky, Russian composer, pianist, and conductor

I've always looked forward to attending worship services, but as a child, I enjoyed church not only because it was spiritually uplifting, but because it allowed me to exercise my favorite activity: singing. Sunday school was another matter. My family almost always arrived late for the Sunday school hour that preceded the worship service because Mom insisted that our dinner must be ready as soon as we returned home. Like other farm families, we referred to the midday meal as dinner rather than lunch. In addition to getting herself and four children dressed and out the door while Dad took care of milking and feeding the livestock, Mom prepared a pot roast and set the table. Year after year, that was her Sunday-morning routine. Like all children, I was born self-centered and remained so for some time. Therefore, I could not comprehend or appreciate how much effort it took for my mother to orchestrate this outcome. I only understood that I didn't like being late for Sunday school.

Even the electric stove that finally replaced our kitchen's wood-burning monster didn't help us get to Sunday school on time despite its build-in timer that turned the oven on and off automatically. But it did ensure that when our family walked through the door at 12:30, we would be greeted by the enticing aroma of roast beef, potatoes, onions, and carrots swimming in beef juice. We never dallied while changing out of our church clothes and scrambling to our assigned seats at the large, rectangular wooden table. We knew the meal would include Mom's homemade bread and a made-from-scratch dessert. All this preparation caused our tardiness for Sunday school, but at least we weren't late for the church service.

I would have preferred to skip Sunday school altogether. The children gathered in a wing added to the sanctuary before my time but was still referred to as "the annex." As I entered late, I felt like an outsider crashing a private party. One energetic teenage girl led the singing, and another played the piano poorly. I thought the songs were babyish and silly. "The b-i-b-l-e, yes that's the book for me..." and "I've got the joy, joy, joy, joy down in my heart" were inadequate expressions of praise to the God I knew. I looked forward to the worship service when I could sing more reverent songs from the hymnal. My favorite hymns were the stately "God of Our Fathers," which I chose many years later for my wedding processional, and "Be Still My Soul" set to Sibelius' beautiful tune, "Finlandia." Such inspirational music transported my spirit beyond the confines of our little country church.

Mom was a good singer who performed solos in church. Often, she received invitations to sing at weddings and funerals. Dad liked to sing, too, but he seldom had time to pursue it. When I was a teenager, Mom told me that, after high school, she enrolled in a secretarial school, but her dream was to go to college and become a professional singer. Like many parents of the time, hers insisted college wasn't for girls. As soon as Mom landed her first secretarial job, she used part of her weekly wage to pay for voice lessons. Whenever she recounted this period of her youth, her demeanor turned wistful. I could see the longing in her eyes.

Often, Marion and I sang duets in church or joined our mother for trios. Eventually, Mom organized a small choir. One evening each week, the group, composed of six to eight aspiring choristers, rehearsed in our living room. Mom never learned to read music, but once Marion developed into an adequate pianist, she managed to teach the parts by rote. I filled in any missing parts, from soprano to tenor. Sometimes I even sang the bass part in my range.

We all looked forward to the annual Christmas cantata when our little choir joined forces with the other two Methodist churches in our pastor's charge. Now we could sing in four-part harmony, under the direction of a public-school choral director and accompanied by the pastor's wife on an electronic organ. The experience was a highlight of the year, and even Dad participated.

Mom and Dad recognized their children's inherent musical talent and were determined to avail us of piano lessons. Marion's studies began when she turned seven. Once a week, Mom, Grandma, and four children piled into Grandma's big Hudson sedan and traveled to Mrs. Wright's house in the next county. Since Mom had not yet earned a driver's license, she depended on her mother-in-law to transport us wherever we needed to go. My tiny grandmother, barely five feet tall, had trouble reaching the pedals. Sitting on a thick pillow allowed her visibility through the windshield but increased her distance from the pedals. With her right foot on the accelerator and her left foot poised on the brake, she assumed a position that resembled standing more than sitting. But off we went.

Marion eagerly anticipated her weekly lessons and loved to practice. Upon arriving at Mrs. Wright's white two-story house with the wide front porch, horseshoe driveway, and large shade trees, Marion jumped out and climbed the front steps alone, carrying her John Thompson Primer with the red cover under one arm and a spiral notebook under the other. I wanted to go inside with her, but I had to wait in the car with Mom, Grandma, and Mark, who was a newborn. While we waited, three-year-old Rodger played with his toy trucks and tractors under a big tree beside the gravel driveway. Sometimes I joined him.

I wanted to play the piano like my sister, but Mom said I must wait until I turned seven. That was still two years away—an eternity. In the meantime, Marion showed me how to find the Middle C position on our old upright piano and taught me how to play the first few pieces in her book by rote.

Marion (Age 2) Loved the Piano
From an Early Age

By the following summer, Mrs. Wright had retired from piano teaching. Mom found a teacher who would come to our house on Saturday mornings. After my sister's lesson, Mrs. Green played her accordion for us and allowed us to try it. She squeezed the air chamber while Marion played a tune on the instrument's vertical keyboard, and I pressed the buttons at the opposite end. Next, four-year-old Rodger took his turn. The sounds emanating from the squeezebox didn't quite resemble music, but the experience was fun. Before leaving for her next appointment, Mrs. Green entertained us with renditions of familiar tunes like "Frère Jacques" and

"Clementine" and invited us to sing along. She said I had a pretty voice and "a good ear," making me proud.

I was deemed old enough to take piano lessons when I reached the second grade. Now there was the third teacher. Miss Everts, a spinster, shared a duplex with her brother and sister-in-law in the Village of Mexico, where we later attended school. Her shingled house was gray, and her piano always wore a blanket of dust. Miss Everts was a tall, slim, austere-looking woman with gray hair. She was one of those adults whose appearance never seemed to change. With her hair pulled back in a bun and her frumpy, long dresses, she looked as old when I took my first lesson at age seven as she did when I took my final lesson as a high school senior. Miss Everts never charged more than a dollar per lesson. Eventually, all four of us studied with her until Rodger and Mark quit piano lessons to participate in sports like football and wrestling.

By the time I took my first lesson, I already knew how to play every song in the John Thompson Primer. I learned them through listening to Marion's practice and reading the finger numbers, a method that worked fine while the music stayed in the Middle C position. I didn't like feeling less than perfect, so I found ways to hide my incompetence, one of which was lying. When Miss Everts asked if Marion had shown me how to play the pieces, I answered, "No." I was determined to convince her I was intelligent and capable, that I had learned them independently. Many years later, I came to understand that teachers don't expect their pupils to arrive already knowledgeable and equipped with skills. The only requirements are a curious mind and a hunger for learning.

Despite her best efforts, Miss Everts failed to inspire me. The John Thompson method did little to invite practicing, and besides, I soon discovered I would rather spend my time singing. Trying her best to encourage me to read the notes on the staff, Miss Everts used a pencil to black out the finger numbers on each page, but I could see through the pencil marks. Perhaps it was desperation that gave me the gift of x-ray vision. For many years, I couldn't seem to concentrate on that other language of lines and circles long enough to make sense of it. I have never been formally diagnosed, but once I became a teacher, I recognized mild symptoms of Attention Deficit Disorder. I tried to practice but grew distracted quickly and bored with the assignment. At the tender age of seven, I needed supervision, motivation, and an imposed schedule. Mom was too busy to reinforce my practice sessions, and Dad was seldom home. Marion became impatient with me and hogged the piano. Somehow, I learned, but the process was tedious. I began to dread my weekly lessons because I felt ill-prepared and anxious. I knew I wanted to be a teacher one day, and as I matured, I resolved to make learning an exciting adventure for my students. They would hunger for more knowledge and new skills because I would nurture each child's inherent gift of wonder.

The instruction continued. Fortunately, my parents never let me entertain the option of quitting, and my intense need for musical expression was powerful enough to endure the tedium. A sporadic practice schedule followed, and I accomplished the basics.

At last, the music became more interesting. As Schumann, Haydn, Beethoven, and Dvorak entered my repertoire, both my interest and attention increased. I grew proficient enough that Marion and I could play duets, but mostly she played, and I sang. Sometimes we both sang, creating harmonious parts and arrangements. We devoured every hymn in the *United Methodist Hymnal* and wore out the thick, red *Family Music Book* that Mom ordered from *Reader's Digest.*

Mexico Academy High School

Throughout high school, my piano lessons were scheduled during study hall. With my parents' permission, the principal allowed me to walk to Miss Evert's house, a few blocks from the school. The walk provided a welcome respite from academia, especially during pleasant weather. Getting outside for a brief period boosted my mood and restored my focus. I could enjoy the sun's rays on my face or watch an autumn breeze swirl dry leaves around my feet. More than a respite, it was a spiritual experience. Sometimes I prayed as I walked, aware of God's presence in nature.

I cannot blame Miss Everts for my stunted progress. Several of my friends fared well under her tutelage. She was a lovely patient woman who tried to teach me, and when she discovered I planned to be a music major in college, she worked diligently to prepare me. Although I minored in piano, it wasn't until my first public-school teaching job that I became a proficient pianist. Dealing with 300 middle school students compelled me to practice enough that I could spot their shenanigans from across the room while playing from a standing position, leading their singing with my voice, and trying to remember all those names. In the case of my piano proficiency, the saying was true that "necessity is the mother of invention."

Despite our humble lifestyle, I was blessed with parents who valued music and recognized my natural gift. They did all they could to nurture my talent and facilitate my music education. My early exposure at church and home laid the foundation for a forty-five-year career as a singer, music educator, and choral conductor. I wouldn't trade those experiences for anything.

Music Is Not God

Music is not God,
but it paves a pathway to God.
Ancient hymns, with their archaic language,
speak what humans of every era long to articulate.
Composers and poets express what we know
but for which we have inadequate words.
Like the infant's cry, filled with raw emotion,
music spews forth from deep within,
leading the way to a higher plane
upon which its Creator waits.

Chapter 16.

Dad's Get-Rich-Quick Scheme

If hard work were such a wonderful thing, surely the rich would have kept it all to themselves.

~(Joseph) Lane Kirkland, US labor union leader who served as President of the AFL-CIO for over sixteen years.

Often, Dad devised get-rich-quick schemes. His goal was to be a millionaire. I suppose he was determined never to experience the Great Depression again. Many of his ideas failed to materialize, but, this time, he had read in *The Wall Street Journal* about chinchillas, those furry rodents with highly valued pelts.

Dad researched until he found a source for purchasing several young chinchillas. Before they arrived, he set up large wire cages in the cellar and bedded them with wood shavings. Then, he ordered special food pellets formulated exclusively for chinchillas. His plan, once the creatures reached adulthood, was to sell them for their plush fur. The wood furnace in the cellar would keep the animals–whose natural habitat was Chile–toasty warm.

Although Mighty Mouse was my favorite cartoon character–because he sang opera arias–I was terrified of rodents. I thought the animals looked no more valuable than the gray squirrels scampering about our yard.

One night, after we had fallen asleep, something strange happened. Music awakened us in the form of raggedy glissandi ascending and descending the piano keyboard. Since the piano was in the living room just beyond my bedroom door, Mom blamed me for the nighttime interruption.

"Lucinda," Mom called, "Stop playing the piano and go back to bed." She always used my given name when scolding me.

"It's not me!" I yelled.

"Marion?"

"Not me!" she shouted from her room at the opposite end of the house.

"Well, whoever it is, go back to bed."

The ill-defined duet continued. After we had endured a few passages in a decidedly impressionistic style, Dad was compelled to get up and check it out. You guessed it. Two of Dad's chinchillas had escaped the cellar and were presenting their concert debut in our living room. As soon as I realized the rodents were loose, I jumped up, slammed my bedroom door, and cowered under the covers.

From his exasperated groaning, I could tell that Dad was not amused to have his sleep interrupted, especially since he had to get up before 5:00 am. But soon, I heard my parents laughing amid scuffling and bumping sounds. These were followed by a few loud Stravinsky-type atonal clusters (i.e., banging and crashing) on the piano. That night, we learned that, unlike squirrels, chinchillas are nocturnal.

Eventually, Mom and Dad corralled the perpetrators and returned them to their cages in the cellar. The house grew quiet again, but not before we engaged in a Walton-family exchange of "good nights," along with Dad's heavy sighs and a few giggles.

The chinchillas never stood a chance of performing at Carnegie Hall. Nor would they contribute their fur to rich people's coats or line Dad's wallet. Weeks later, Dad's scheme ended abruptly when a chimney fire caused the cellar to fill with deadly smoke.

Chapter 17.

Mom and the Wedding Cake

The most dangerous food is wedding cake.

~ James Thurber, American cartoonist, author, humorist, journalist, and playwright

Once each month, Mom met with the Ladies Home Bureau (LHB). Through the LHB, she learned how to decorate cakes, hoping to start filling orders for birthday cakes. Ready to embark on a new career, she practiced making intricate roses out of icing, carefully positioning them on a cardboard prototype. I enjoyed observing the process, especially when she allowed me to scrape the bowls and lick the spoons.

Mom started her little side business by baking and decorating birthday cakes for relatives, neighbors, and church friends. Soon she equipped her spare country kitchen with various ingredients and implements, including cake pans of different shapes and sizes. Mom didn't use commercial cake mixes. She made all her baked goods from "scratch," measuring, sifting, and mixing by hand. After baking the batter in the oven of her wood-burning stove, she assembled the layers on a rigid round cardboard base wrapped in aluminum foil and covered with a large paper doily resembling delicate lace. A sugary layer of pure white icing held it all together.

When the time came to decorate her creations, Mom divided the remaining frosting into individual bowls. Using only four food dyes in primary colors, she mixed whatever tint or hue was needed. After scooping each mixture into an icing bag, she grasped it with both hands and, squeezing firmly, piped the icing through small metal cones affixed to the bags. Each cone had a unique opening. One shape produced flowers, another formed leaves, and others created grooved, woven, or cylindrical edgings. Mom's decorating kit provided endless possibilities for festive adornments. Expertly, she made scenes that were either elegant or whimsical, depending upon the occasion. Her final act was to write the birthday honoree's name in cursive across the top layer. This task required a steady hand, but she learned to center the greeting perfectly after much practice.

To her repertoire, Mom added cakes for other occasions, including baby showers, bridal showers, and retirement parties. One day, she agreed to fill her first order for a wedding cake. My mother explained to her children that this project would encompass two full workdays during which rambunctious observers would not be permitted in the kitchen. She seemed to have forgotten we had to traverse the kitchen to reach the bathroom, the second-floor bedrooms, and the backyard. With the wedding date approaching, I noticed that Mom was growing tense. From her increasing impatience with us kids and her frequent sighs, I sensed she had second thoughts about her proposed career.

When Dad arrived for supper, Mom had mixed, poured, and baked six perfect layers, setting them on wire racks to cool. The kitchen table was covered with flour, sugar, shortening, dirty mixing bowls, spoons, and measuring cups, and the dining room table overflowed with her latest sewing project. Not only was there no indication of supper preparations, but there was no place to eat.

Mom prepared a meager meal of grilled cheese sandwiches and Campbell's tomato soup for us to consume picnic-style on the living room floor, drinking our soup from mugs. To this day, it remains one of my favorite meals. While Dad washed the supper dishes, Mom supervised bath time and tucked us into bed. Usually, she shared songs and prayers at bedtime, but we had to be satisfied with a hug and a quick peck on the cheek that night.

The following day, I descended the stairs early to find my mother bustling in the kitchen. She had risen before dawn, in time to feed Dad and send him on his way to his farm chores. Now, she faced a messy kitchen and naked cake yet to be assembled and decorated. I watched in awe as my mother, her forehead wrinkled in determination, prepared a generous batch of white icing. After combining numerous boxes of confectioner's sugar, a small can of Crisco shortening, and a generous measure of vanilla extract, she whipped the mixture into a fluffy mound. Magically, she fashioned hundreds of roses, one petal at a time, and set them on waxed paper to harden.

"Can I help...I mean, *may* I help?" I asked.

She smiled at my correction and said, "Not with the cake, but I'll have plenty of jobs for you later." Mom explained she would assemble the double-layer sections into three graduated tiers. "The whole cake will stand three feet tall, and I'll cover it in pure white icing before I start decorating," she said. I could tell she enjoyed this artistic part of the process by the excited tone in her voice and her animated description.

"What time is the wedding?" I asked.

"It's scheduled for five," she said, "and by four-thirty, I must deliver the cake, remove the reinforcements, add the topper, and surround the base with ivy garlands." Blowing air noisily through pursed lips, she wiped her brow with the back of her hand, then slid both palms along her icing-smeared apron.

Mom told me to wake Marion, who liked to sleep late on Saturday mornings. After three attempts, I succeeded in rousing my grumpy, grumbling sister. No sooner had she descended the stairs, rubbing her half-open eyelids, than Mom began issuing orders. She instructed Marion to make oatmeal and pour cups of milk for our brothers and charged me with setting the card table Dad had erected in the living room. Mom prayed aloud, "Please don't let the boys wake up early today."

"You girls go ahead and eat," Mom said. "Then feed your brothers and help them get dressed. I laid out their clothes last night." Chores made me feel like I mattered and that my household contributions were significant. Now I felt useful.

Marion complained about being assigned hard jobs because she was the oldest, but she completed her tasks in the end. Mom assembled the layers and frosted the entire cake by lunchtime despite the expected interruptions in a mother's typical day—spilled milk, potty-training mishaps, and refereeing sibling squabbles. She had spread the icing so smoothly that her structure resembled fine porcelain.

"Girls, I need you to keep your brothers out of my hair until naptime," Mom said. "Take them outside to play running games so they'll be tired for their naps." After breakfast, Marion and I planned the morning's activities: games of Tree Tag, Mother-May-I, and Hide-and-Seek in the front yard. We pulled our brothers' tricycles off the back porch, so they could ride up and down the long horseshoe-shaped driveway again and again. We agreed that if we could convince Rodger and Mark that they were construction workers operating bulldozers and backhoes, the boys would stick with the activity longer. Before we had cleared the table and washed the breakfast dishes, the boys, ages six and three, were nagging us to start the promised adventures.

Mom remained on schedule despite a few bumps and scrapes requiring her brief attention. When we returned to the makeshift bakery, we found she had adorned the cake with roses, added delicate leaves, and edged each tier with trailing garlands of twisted cord fashioned entirely of icing. I thought the cake looked dazzling, and I imagined the scene where the bride and groom cut the first piece and fed it to each other lovingly.

After lunch, we settled our brothers for their afternoon naps, and Mom issued our next instructions. "As soon as I finish the decorations, you'll need to help me get the cake into the car. It'll be heavy, so we'll have to work together." With Dad's help, Mom had prepared a unique plywood platform for the backseat of our Nash Ambassador. She designed her invention to provide a level, stable surface. "You'll sit up front with your brothers," she told me. "Marion, you'll sit in the back to make sure the cake doesn't tip or slide." I was relieved to be spared the responsibility of keeping Mom's *magnum opus* safe during what proved a harrowing eight-mile trip to town. Mom said the car windows must remain closed to prevent damage from wind and flying insects. Cars were not air-conditioned in those days, but fortunately it was a cool summer day.

With the masterpiece completed, the moment for transfer arrived. Mom had inserted vertical bamboo skewers through the layers to hold them together. She explained that, when we arrived at the reception venue, she would remove the rods and patch the entry points with extra icing she had packed in a Mason jar. Carefully, she slid the cake's cardboard base onto the plywood to convey its precious cargo to the waiting car.

According to plan, I went first, opening doors and checking to ensure the cake remained level. Marion and Mom, positioned at opposite ends of the platform, lifted and carried the heavy load with great care as I directed Mom's backward movements out the kitchen door, through the mudroom, and down the rear porch steps. Aware that one false move would prove disastrous, I opened the car door and guided my mother as she slid fanny-first across the backseat and leveled the platform before releasing her side and slipping out the opposite door.

With our mission completed, we returned to the house and waited for two unsuspecting boys to awaken from their naps. Mom collapsed onto a kitchen chair, covered in sweat and flour, her arms hanging limp at her sides. But within minutes, she popped up and bolted out the back door. I ran to the window to see her checking the car's interior temperature to ensure it hadn't caused icing to melt or tiers to slide. She checked again and again and again. Until that momentous encounter with the wedding cake business, I had no idea it was so time-consuming and stressful. Secretly, I hoped my mother wouldn't accept any more orders.

Mom had just enough time to tidy the kitchen and change her clothes before my brothers awakened at three-thirty. That's when we sprang into action. I packed graham crackers and juice for the boys to consume in the car. Marion helped them with their shoes and shepherded them out the back door. After Mom's final inspection of the backseat cargo, we set out.

The trip proved even more nerve-racking than the loading process. Mom drove so slowly that she forced other drivers to ride her rear bumper and honk at her with impatient annoyance. Then, as soon as an opportunity presented itself, they gunned their engines and flew past, looking enraged. I lowered my head in embarrassment as Marion shook her index finger and shouted–through a closed window–at each infuriated driver. Our mother resembled a madwoman, with her white knuckles gripping the steering wheel and wide eyes fixed on the road ahead. Committed to her singular mission, she seemed oblivious to her surroundings, except for that enormous tower of confection balanced on the backseat. Every few minutes, she asked Marion to report its status. After the fourth inquiry, my exasperated sister said, "Trust me, Mom. I'll tell you if it shifts as much as an inch."

"Are you sure? Does it look like the icing is melting?"

"No, it's fine. Please hurry and get there before I have an angina attack!" At Marion's unexpected comment, Mom burst into laughter. Her sudden change of mood incited the boys to fits of giggling.

"Where did you hear that expression?" she asked as her grip on the steering wheel relaxed a bit.

"I don't know," answered Marion. "Are we there yet? Just tell me we're there."

For the remainder of the trip, Rodger and Mark, attempting to prolong the welcome levity, called out, "Gina tack! Gina tack!" while I tried, without success, to shush them.

Once we arrived in town, Mom maneuvered numerous curves and turned corners cautiously before pulling into the restaurant's rear parking lot, choosing the space closest to the building. "Whew! Right on time," she said, releasing a huge sigh.

"Okay, Lu," she directed me, "you stay in the car with your brothers. Marion, help me take the cake inside." I held my breath until the heavy load disappeared through the restaurant's service entrance.

I was finishing a game of I Spy with my fidgety little brothers when Marion returned to report, "Mission accomplished." She collected Mom's bag of touch-up implements and disappeared into the building once more.

At last, our mother emerged from the restaurant. Her face registered both fatigue and relief. In her right hand, she waved a crisp fifty-dollar bill. Ignoring Mark's cries of, "Mommy, Mommy!" she slipped into the driver's seat, rested her head on the steering wheel, and muttered, "It'll be a cold day in hell—"

"Mother!" Marion and I interrupted in shocked unison. Never had we heard as much as a mild expletive from the mouth of our prim-and-proper mother. She had taught us that "stupid" and "shut up" were curse words. Indeed, she had never uttered the word "hell" before, especially in the presence of her young children.

Our mother had just delivered her first–and last–wedding cake.

Chapter 18.

Lazy Hazy Days

Ah, summer, what power you have to make us suffer and like it.

~Russell Baker, American author

Summers on the farm shaped my most pleasant childhood memories. Before we were old enough to help with chores, my siblings and I played outside all day, going indoors only to use the bathroom or refuel. We managed to investigate every copse, brook, and meadow. At times, I wondered why we were allowed so much freedom to explore the potentially dangerous areas of a 400-acre property, but I never asked for fear of putting ideas into our parents' heads. My cautious, protective mother stayed busy inside the house, and Dad worked incessantly on the adjacent farm or in the woods, felling trees and splitting logs for winter fuel. Perhaps Mom trusted Marion, the oldest, to keep us safe, or maybe she thought her fear-laden warnings were enough to deter us from risky behavior.

Sunshine was my remedy for every ailment. I savored it like precious drops of water from a desert traveler's canteen. The sun's rays healed my itchy skin and relieved my melancholy. Although I tried to be entertaining and light-hearted, I was not a happy, carefree child. Instead, I felt anxious and morose much of the time. The hours I spent inside my head generated a lively imagination but also fueled all sorts of worst-case scenarios. It wasn't until middle age that I was diagnosed

Loomis Kids' Parade

with clinical depression and began to receive treatment. I'm convinced my father also suffered this ailment. Because he grew up in a generation that perceived mental illness as a weakness, he couldn't acknowledge his condition. Nor did he ever receive treatment. It saddens me when I consider how much better the quality of his life might have been. I've heard it said that depression is "anger turned inward." My father and I spent much of our lives angry at ourselves and negatively affecting our loved ones through criticism and complaining.

But, when I was a child, lazy summer days temporarily reduced my despondency and relieved my eczema. The sunshine and pleasant breezes provided a welcome reprieve, allowing me to enjoy activities with my siblings like mock parades in the front yard under the shade of mature maple trees. Especially after watching the annual Fourth of July parade in the nearby Village of Mexico, we'd march around and around, shoulders back, knees lifted high, with our homespun flags fashioned from sticks and fabric scraps left from Mom's sewing projects. Various sized pots and pans or empty boxes served as drums that we tapped with wooden-spoon drumsticks, and fallen twigs became flutes or clarinets.

Summer's additional hours of daylight meant we could stay up later. My siblings and I filled the hours from dawn to dusk with games of Tree-tag, Mother-May-I, or cowboys-and-Indians. As we grew older, baseball occupied most of our waking hours until harvest time required our help. Since rolling hills, open fields, and woodlands surrounded our farmhouse, we never experienced a shortage of space for any game. If we ventured beyond the yard, slipping under the electric wire fences, our challenge was to avoid stepping in cowpies that littered the pastures. But even cowpies couldn't dissuade us from our adventures.

Beyond the chicken coop behind the house was a large pond surrounded by marshland nestled in a ring of dense woods. Dad called the pond a lake and convinced us it was so deep it was bottomless. He was sure a meteorite had created it. He told us we could play in the woods, but we must not go near the lake. "Many a cow wandered into the marsh, got sucked into the mud, and washed into the lake, never to be seen again," he cautioned. I don't know about my siblings, but his warning was enough to deter me. I played in the woods but kept my distance from the water. Besides, we lived close enough to Lake Ontario to spend an occasional Saturday there picnicking, swimming, and enjoying the sandy beach at Fair Haven State Park or Selkirk Shores State Park.

Each spring, as soon as the last snow melted, the still-damp canvas surrounding our pond burst with trilliums, some red, some white. One year, my siblings and I bent down and picked as many of the woodland beauties as our arms could hold. We ran to the house to present our floral gifts to our mother, but sadly before we reached the back porch, every blossom had withered atop its wilted stem. Mom explained to her disappointed children that trilliums weren't fond of leaving their natural habitat and that it was best to enjoy their beauty where they grew. She placed the stems in water, but our bouquets failed to revive. We never picked the trilliums again.

The pine plantation across the road, up the hill, beyond the cornfield, was an inviting place to play. Devoid of underbrush, this woodland with its towering pines afforded ample space for running, playing, and imagining. All but the most prominent rocks had been cleared before Dad planted the trees in neat rows. We loved to explore these woods, climbing atop the few remaining boulders to act out scenes from *The Davy Crockett Show* or build secret shelters beneath fallen branches and pine straw. Sometimes, I'd lie on the needle-padded earth and gaze through the tall swaying treetops to study the clouds and enjoy nature's symphony. Even now, if I close my eyes, I can hear the wind whistling through the high branches and crows cawing in the cornfield nearby.

Occasionally, Mom prepared a picnic lunch for us. She would spread an old, worn blanket under one of the nut trees in the side yard near the raspberry patch. Sometimes we morphed into pioneers-heading-west-on-a-wagon-train. Setting up camp required circling the wagons, feeding the horses, gathering firewood, and cooking over an open fire. Fallen tree branches or broken broomsticks and rake handles became galloping horses with feed-sack saddles, and twigs served as make-believe cigarettes. Nothing on the farm was discarded, no matter how seemingly useless.

Mom insisted that smoking cigarettes was sinful, but the cowboys we watched on TV smoked Marlboros or Lucky Strikes, except our hero, Roy Rogers, the singing cowboy. Sometimes, people told Dad he resembled Roy Rogers, an impression he enjoyed because Roy was considered handsome. Dad took pride in his thick, wavy brown hair and slim, muscled physique. Occasionally, Roy Rogers fans would ask Dad for his autograph in public settings. Dad encouraged this mistaken identity by wearing a string tie and western belt buckle whenever we went to town.

When my brothers reached nine or ten, they spent most of their summers

Mark, Age 5, Plowing with the Horse Team

helping Dad and Grandpa with the farm chores. Mark dreamed of becoming a farmer one day, but Rodger planned to become the CEO of General Motors. Marion loved the outdoors, enjoyed the animals, and preferred farm work to housework. She often accompanied Dad and the boys to the dairy barn. For me, the price was too high. I couldn't risk spending the next several days wheezing and scratching my skin until it bled. Summers in New York State were too brief to spend in misery.

On warm rainy evenings, Mom sometimes took a bottle of Prell shampoo outside to let us wash our hair, rinsing it in the soft rainwater. We'd strip down to our underwear and run wildly through the rain shower until our hair was squeaky clean. We enjoyed the tickle of wet grass on our bare feet and the freedom of staying up later than usual to indulge in activities apart from the school-day routine. Once we were clean, Mom wrapped each play-weary child in a bath towel and read us a bedtime story on the steps of our small, covered front porch. During such times I sensed that Mom tried to enjoy motherhood. Still, perhaps the overwhelming challenges of raising four children with few modern conveniences sapped her joy as it depleted her energy.

One summer day, Marion and I were exploring the barn, not Grandpa's dairy barn "down home," but the deserted building on our property "up home." Before we moved there, the acreage occupied by our house, barn, and various outbuildings had been an independent farm. Dad used the structurally sound but shabby barn to store tools, lawnmowers, snow removal equipment, old cars, and, later, Grandma's antiques. We loved investigating the interior, searching for treasures, or acting out scenes from our myriad impromptu plays. The old hayloft was especially appealing, with its vast open space and beams from which to swing like Tarzan. My predictable spells of wheezing and sneezing were worth it. Almost.

During one rummage, Marion and I found a pile of heavy, pressed boards left from some construction project before our time. The panels—about four feet square—were both thin and sturdy, perfect for building a playhouse. The planning began in earnest, and our primitive construction followed. We carried board after board to the center of the backyard, where the ground was level, and placed them in formation. Next, we hauled stumps of pre-split firewood from the woodpile to form supports for our edifice. Standing the wood chunks on end, we placed some inside each wall and some outside. We discovered that overlapping the boards increased their sturdiness and allowed us to create doorways.

Soon a room emerged, then another and another. With additional boards, we covered the entire structure with a flat roof. It didn't matter that we couldn't stand inside or that our mansion was precarious and windowless. Our apartments were cozy, and we took pride in constructing them through ingenuity and labor. We personalized our units by adding simple furnishings from

The Deserted Barn on Our Property

the "big" house: a few chairs, a blanket or two, and plenty of dolls. While I made mud cookies in my kitchen, Marion found some empty clay flowerpots stacked on the back porch. She filled them with soil from one of our property's many flowerbeds and "borrowed" a few marigolds to plant in each container.

With the stage set, we became neighboring housewives who visited each other's homes for tea and cookies. We cared for our babies and engaged in chores we had observed in the real house: sweeping floors, preparing meals, baking bread, washing dishes, doing laundry, and changing diapers. Being homemakers and mothers was what we knew. Our television models were June Cleaver of *Leave it to Beaver*, Ruth Martin of *Lassie*, and Margaret Anderson of *Father Knows Best*–quintessential housewives. Our mother, aunts, and grandmothers served as real-life role models. None of them had a career outside the home while raising their families. As I reflect on those girlhood days in the 1950s, I remember the insecurities I often felt then and later as a young woman. I recall the conflict that existed in my thinking. Yes, I wanted marriage and children, but I also wanted an education and a career. How was that combination possible? Would I have to sacrifice one for the other?

Women still had few opportunities available to them without a fight. If they wanted to work outside the home, societal expectations created guilt about neglecting their families. Tradition limited their career aspirations to nursing, teaching, or secretarial work. If they wanted only a career and no children, guilt accompanied that choice. Fortunately for girls of my generation, the sixties were just around the corner, an era when pioneers like Betty Friedan, Germaine Greer, and Gloria Steinem, building upon the earlier work of suffragists, began to challenge stereotypical feminine roles in ways that garnered notice. They brought attention to important issues and challenged women's traditional roles. It wasn't until the 1970s that I acknowledged my right to equal respect, equal opportunities, and the same life choices as men.

But summer was not the season to carry emotional burdens or dwell on issues associated with adulthood. Childhood summers on the farm were for sunshine, exploration, and fantasy.

God is in the Wind

God is in the rush of wind that wakes me in the night,
God is in the clamorous crows that rise in frantic flight,
To signal, "stay away" or "come and share abundant yield."
God is there when lightning streaks across a golden field.

God is in the morning drops upon each blade of green;
in beams of sunlight filtered through my bedroom window screen.
How can one not see God's face etched upon a leaf,
or pouring through the lonely tears of mourners wracked with grief?

I know God's presence all around and deep within my soul.
All of life becomes a prayer when God is in control.
God's Spirit is electric, His message pure love;
His children see His face when they lift their gaze above.

'Mid earthly pain and loneliness, I cry, "Come fill my heart!"
Teach me how to do your will and carry out my part.
Like wind and crows, leaves and dew, grass and lightning, too,
I sing with all creation, "Lord, my life belongs to you!"

Chapter 19.

A Wedding to Remember

A grand and lavish wedding does not guarantee a happy marriage.

~Rajesh Bohan, Editor-in-Chief of *The Dawn Journal*

One spring day in 1956, Mom announced that her cousin would get married in New York City. She said Marion and I would be allowed to attend the wedding. For two naïve country girls who seldom had left the farm, it promised to be a once-in-a-lifetime experience. When Mom added that our little brothers were too young for such a fancy affair, this seven-year-old felt ever-so-grown up.

I learned that Mom's cousin was to marry a Catholic girl. My childish logic deduced that Catholic must mean rich because Mom said the wedding would be a large lavish affair in one of Manhattan's most elaborate cathedrals. The reception would take place at the Waldorf Astoria Hotel.

We would need new clothes.

My mother started sewing immediately and spent every waking moment fashioning our elegant matching dresses of blue organza. She took us shopping for patent-leather shoes, fluffy petticoats, white gloves, and Easter-style hats with blue velvet ribbons streaming down the back. Marion and I could hardly wait for our exciting new experience. But I felt anxious, too, since I was unaccustomed to settings more sophisticated than our tiny country church with its peeling paint and rickety altar.

Finally, the anticipated day arrived. Mom packed our outfits in tissue paper with Dad's pristine suit and her new dress of lavender taffeta, two more products of her Singer sewing machine.

After Dad studied a map with meticulous consideration, we piled into our Nash Ambassador and headed for The Big Apple.

After a three-hundred-mile drive that took most of the day, we arrived in The City. I was overwhelmed by the tall buildings, unfamiliar odors, dense traffic, and deafening noise. Amid honking horns and wailing sirens, hordes of people scurried in all directions. I almost heard them chattering, "I'm late, I'm late! For a very important date."

Dad located the hotel where we would spend the night and parked in an underground garage. The hotel wasn't anything like I had imagined. It was old and musty, with no elevator to carry us to the third floor. We climbed and climbed until we reached the dingy room and tiny bathroom the four of us would share. One window overlooked the busy street in front of our hotel and the other a dark, narrow alley. A double bed, two cots, and a chair completed the room's sparse furnishings. I questioned my mother's interpretation of "lavish" and "elaborate" and was relieved to learn this hotel was not the Waldorf Astoria.

Mom had brought a box of Wheaties for our breakfast and a small, covered pail of milk. She opened a window and set the bucket on the sill, so the cool night air would keep it from souring before morning. She also had packed bowls, cups, spoons, and a small electric percolator. I didn't have to ask why we couldn't eat breakfast in the hotel's dining room, nor would I risk precipitating one of Dad's speeches about how expensive everything was. Having lived through the Great Depression, he was frugal to a fault.

Sleep eluded me, partly because I was excited about the wedding but primarily because of the blinking neon signs and relentless traffic noise. After tossing and turning for half the night, I devised a plan. I tip-toed to the bathroom, tore off pieces of toilet tissue, and, stuffing them in my ears, returned to my cot. I pulled the covers over my head and finally fell asleep.

When Mom shook me awake the following day, I felt groggy. As I slumped over the cot's edge, trying to open my eyes, I removed the tissue plugs from my ears. Mom, Dad, and Marion enjoyed a good laugh at my ingenuity, and I pretended not to revel in the attention.

We ate our cereal—mine without milk. Not only was I allergic to milk, but I couldn't stomach the taste, especially at room temperature. Mom washed the dishes in the bathtub while my sister and I donned our beautiful new frocks and accessories. I wished my patent leather shoes were strapless like Marion's and had little heels like hers, but I grudgingly accepted Mom's explanation of why older girls were permitted to wear grown-up clothes sooner than their younger sisters.

My mother looked exquisite in her lavender taffeta dress with a peek-a-boo back and tailored matching jacket. She had worn pink, spongy curlers in her hair all night, and now the shiny brunette curls emerged from under her pillbox hat, framing her pretty face.

Dad had planned to wear his one-and-only navy-blue uniform, the suit he saved for weddings and funerals, but Mom insisted on making him a seersucker suit for the occasion. Mom straightened Dad's tie, gave one final tug at the seams of her fine handiwork, and pecking him on the cheek, told him he was handsome. How different he looked without his usual farmer's coveralls, denim cap, and knee-high boots! He smelled good, too. Usually, I avoided contact with my father because he smelled like farm animals, their feed, and their waste. Now, I decided that, if invited, I would gladly accept his hugs and sit on his lap.

We re-packed our overnight bags and headed downstairs to the gloomy lobby to check out. As Dad was paying our bill, I overheard the clerk mention, with a chuckle, something about an Easter parade, but I caught only the tail-end of his comment. I was too busy watching the other guests who seemed wealthy and important.

Dad located our car in the garage, loaded our bags in the trunk, and drove across town after checking a city map. Along the way, he complained about the traffic. "Why would anyone want to live in a big city? It's so noisy, dirty, and crowded!" Mom tried to read the map while placating Dad, pointing out sights to her girls, and reminding us to be on our best behavior. Finally, we located the mammoth Gothic cathedral where the ceremony would occur.

We had arrived an hour early, giving us time to walk about the grounds and appreciate the impressive edifice that filled a whole city block. When Marion and I spotted the austere stone building, we were held spellbound by its grandeur. Dad mumbled something about rich people showing off, but I paid little attention. I was engrossed in my fantasy of princess brides, prancing horses, and gilt carriages like I had seen on *The Wonderful World of Disney*. I spotted a lush, manicured lawn with elaborate fountains, stone benches, and colorful flowerbeds inside the stone-walled courtyard. Sunlight squeezed through the leafy tree limbs on that perfect summer morning, spotlighting a verdant stage below.

Soon a long white limousine pulled up to the curb. Only in television movies had I seen such a posh vehicle. Out stepped the most exquisite bride! If truth be told, her long face with its sizable aquiline nose wasn't especially pretty, but her gown with its yards of luxurious fabric, long train, and filmy veil made up for any deficit in the bride's countenance. A sparkling tiara like the one in my recurring dream held the veil in place. As the young woman arranged her ample skirt, I noticed the hem retained its perfect circular shape with the help of a hoop that bobbed to-and-fro when she walked. I wondered how she had managed to squeeze it through the car door.

Next, the bridesmaids alighted, one after the other, carrying generous bouquets of white roses and trailing greenery. Marion elbowed my arm as if to say, "Do you see what I see?" As six identically garbed attendants exited, we stood in silent amazement, and a sea of blue chiffon poured onto the sidewalk. Six satin headpieces balanced atop the women's matching up-dos. Like water billowing from a fountain, blue netting erupted from each headpiece, fastened with a sprig of baby's breath. As graceful blue waves flowed up the steps, disappearing into the church, I was sure I would never again witness a more enchanting vision.

Once we stepped inside, Marion and I could scarcely contain our wonderment. Surely, we had entered the set of one of Ziegfeld's elaborate, over-the-top stage revues we sometimes watched on our black-and-white TV. But this scene was in living color. I peeked from behind Mom's skirt into the endless nave, feeling dwarfed by the high arched ceiling with its flying buttresses. The entire cavernous space was awash in white flowers, flickering candles, and billowy white bows. When a tuxedoed usher offered his arm to my mother, Dad fell in step behind the pair. In a moment of panic, I realized no one had briefed me on proper etiquette for such a formal occasion. Would ushers escort Marion and me? Should we follow our parents or wait for an usher to return for us? Would Dad give us a signal? Fortunately, my sister—always the acting cruise director—grabbed my arm and nudged me forward.

Once our family had settled at the end of a pew about halfway down the long aisle, I discovered I couldn't see past the extravagant hats adorning every woman in front of us. So, Mom allowed me to stand in the aisle. "Stay close," she warned, pulling me snugly against the side of the pew. Soon glorious pipe organ music poured from every crevice of the sacred space. Again, I stood in awe, mouth agape. "Close your mouth," Mom whispered, tapping my chin.

Marion giggled into her cupped hands and rolled her eyes as if to say, "You're such a dweeb!" Before I had a chance to scowl at her, the music halted. I jerked my head toward the altar to see what was happening. There I observed the tuxedoed groom and four groomsmen moving into place. At the rear entrance, the bridesmaids stood in perfect pairs, waiting for a signal. Next, two ushers walked the long aisle toward the back, unrolling a white cloth runner along the floor. "Squeak, squeak," it sang as it passed row after row of guests. Once the ushers completed their task, the music resumed, and the pairs of bridesmaids processed in seamless synchrony—step-touch, step-touch, step-touch. I was tempted to reach out and graze the inviting blue clouds as they passed, but I resisted, sensing that such a bold move could jeopardize my prime vantage point. I was content to remain an invisible observer.

Only the flower girl took notice of me. As she and the tiny ring-bearer passed, the girl smiled and dropped some rose petals on my shiny new shoes. I responded with a slight wave of my gloved fingers and felt almost like I belonged in this opulent setting for the first time since arriving. When the miniature couple reached the front, the music stopped again. Now the bride and the man I assumed was her father appeared in the arched entrance at the rear of the church. An open door behind them framed their silhouettes in halos of sunlight. As if they had rehearsed it, the congregants stood with a unison "whoosh," and the music resumed with increased grandeur. Now I recognized the tune as "Here Comes the Bride."

With the bride's face covered in white netting, she was a lovely sight. Awash in multi-colored sunbeams, she and her proud escort began their long slow procession toward the chancel. When the bride's skirt brushed past me, I hugged the pew to prevent being knocked over by its voluminous fabric and swaying hoop.

Finally, the couple reached its destination, and the interminable service began—Mom called it a Mass. It was boring, mainly because the priest spoke in a language I didn't understand. The chant-like singing was strange and unfamiliar, causing my seven-year-old imagination to stray to thoughts of my future wedding. I would be the most beautiful bride! My train would flow for miles, my veil trimmed with delicate lace. Masses of flowers and cascading greenery would fill the church. Oh! The church—that sad little country chapel with an aisle so short that, even if we marched very slowly, my father and I would reach the rickety altar rail before the organist finished her fanfare introduction. Never mind. I'd have plenty of time to work out the details.

I climbed down from the pew to reclaim my appointed observation post. Halfway through the Mass, a collective gasp jolted me from my reverie. I glanced around to see what was happening and noticed women covering their eyes and snickering into their gloved hands.

When the bride and groom knelt at the altar for the most dignified part of the service, no one could have prepared for the scene before them. The wedding planner had not predicted what would happen to the bride's hoop-skirted gown when she dropped to her knees in prayer. There, encased in a perfect round frame for all her guests to see, was the bride's silky white underwear, garters and all. Frantically, she reached behind, trying to lower the hoop. I stared aghast at the sight, unable to fathom how a bride might ever recover from such a horrifying turn of events on her most important day.

With their heads bowed and eyes closed, the wedding party stood oblivious to the bride's embarrassing display. But, as soon as the priest uttered "Amen" and heads bobbed up, all denial vanished. Now, the maid of honor and her court scrambled into position, trying to salvage whatever dignity remained. Two attempts to lower the bride's skirt failed. Each time the hoop sprang back to its cylindrical shape. As a bewildered priest tried to carry on, the attendants formed a barrier of blue chiffon around the bride's backside. At last, decorum was restored until attention shifted to the aisle where a seven-year-old girl stood gripping the pew and shaking.

I could never explain how the urge managed to possess me so completely. The shaking started in my toes and worked its way up in powerful giggles. With a muffled slap, both hands flew to my mouth, but there was no containing it. Like Mount Vesuvius spewing lava, gales of laughter erupted, echoing off the marble floor. Marion snorted into her palms, but our mortified parents were not amused. Mom pulled me toward her, and, covering my mouth, pushed my face onto her lap. When, at last, I regained enough composure to look up, the moment had passed, but not before I had thoroughly embarrassed my parents.

That was the moment the fantasy of my wedding took a detour. I resolved that the skirt of my perfect princess gown would not include a hoop, and my guest list most certainly would not include unpredictable children.

***

The reception hall evoked an even greater marvel than the awe-inspiring church. The Waldorf Astoria's ballroom had been transformed into a magical fairyland. Tiny, white lights and garlands of greenery covered with blue netting draped the upper level's banister. Wreaths of white roses surrounding white globed candles adorned dozens of round tables. The white, double-layered tablecloths were gathered upward at four points and fastened with white roses and blue ribbons. Likewise, the chairs were draped in fabric with roses and ribbon cascading down the backs. This time when my jaw dropped, Mom was too astonished to notice.

One of many waiters, dressed in a black waistcoat, shiny black trousers, stiff white shirt, and bow tie, led my family around the central dance floor to a table where he held Mom's chair, then Marion's and mine, in turn. My thoughts drifted to Cinderella's ball—with one crucial revision. I, of course, was the main character of my fantasy. Glancing toward the dance floor, I saw myself waltzing with a handsome prince whose eyes stared adoringly into mine. I whirled across the smooth parquet floor, my glass slippers barely touching the tiles. My white, bejeweled, gown floated back and forth as my graceful partner spun me around the open space. Suddenly, Mom broke my reverie when she snapped at Marion, "Don't drink that!" My sister had lifted a delicate crystal glass to her lips.

"But I'm thirsty."

"That's Champagne!" Mom responded.

"What's Champagne?" I asked.

Mom's answers were almost always insufficient. "It's not for children," came her vague response. It was yet another instance in which I hoped that one day I would be invited to join the sorority known as "adulthood" when, at last, all secrets would be revealed.

"Would the young ladies care for a ginger ale?" inquired an observant waiter.

"Yes," Mom answered for the 'young ladies,' "and bring him some." She flashed a glare of disdain at Dad, who was sneaking sips of the bubbly liquid. Mom, a devout Methodist, had been raised in a temperate home where any form of alcohol was considered the devil's brew. Usually, Dad followed suit to keep the peace, but the atypical twinkle in his eye told me he didn't think this occasion was usual. As soon as something averted Mom's attention, Dad sneaked another sip and winked at Marion, who giggled. I basked in this rare playful side of my father.

By the time the food came, I felt ravenous. That bowl of dry Wheaties had long since digested. Nothing could have prepared me for the feast set before me, course after delectable course. A bowl of clear broth introduced the meal. Mom, who had taken home economics in high school, said it was consommé, but it reminded me of the bullion she gave me whenever my tummy hurt. A crisp endive salad with cherry tomatoes followed the soup course, accompanied by scrumptious yeast rolls with whipped butter. I could have made an entire meal of those rolls. Next came the entrée, and I could scarcely believe my eyes. The waiters served each of some three hundred guests an entire Cornish hen! Mounds of creamy mashed potatoes, cornbread stuffing, and julienne vegetables surrounded the perfectly roasted birds. Each plate was a feast for a king…or a princess. I had not yet spotted the wedding cake in the far corner of the ballroom, or I would have saved room for dessert.

After finishing our dinner-sized lunches, Mom said it was time for us "girls" to locate the ladies' room. That's when I spotted the sugary mountain. It stood taller than a Christmas tree with four double-tiers of sculpted cake covered with white icing. Roses and leaves formed from icing adorned each tier. On the top layer stood the smiling wedding couple—a delicate china bride and her toy groom—ready to live happily ever after. Marion and I had to crane our necks toward the ceiling to study the tiny figurines. A round table supported the exquisite work of art. It was covered to the floor in white linens and pink netting with a garland of ivy and real pink roses. "Wow!" I whispered as I passed. My jaw was getting quite a workout that day.

The ladies' room was equally impressive with its marble grandeur and monogrammed cloth towels. Our trio returned to the ballroom to see waiters serving the cake. Despite my full stomach, the size of my slice was disappointing. In my seven-year-old opinion, it could have been twice as large with much more icing, but it was as delicious as I had anticipated. I wished I could take some home for later.

Soon the orchestra moved into place and the dancing began. First, the bride and groom took the floor. As they stared into each other's eyes, they seemed deliriously happy and madly in love. I noticed the bride had removed the hoop from her skirt, ensuring no further wardrobe mishaps. Next, the bride danced with her father. Finally, the attendants joined the celebration, and soon the large dance floor filled with revelers who seemed at ease in this formal setting. I supposed that, when I grew up, I would instinctively know how to act and what to say in social settings such as this, but throughout the day, I felt out of my element, hoping no one would notice or speak to me. Nothing in my brief, sheltered, rural life had prepared me for this foreign, but thoroughly enchanting, affair.

Marion and I shared a shocked expression when our hay-seed father asked Mom to dance. We had never observed our parents in a sophisticated setting and were surprised to discover they knew how to dance. Mom looked happier than we had ever seen her as Dad guided her gracefully through the crowd with ease.

More surprises awaited us when Dad invited each of us, in turn, to join him on the dance floor. Swirling and twirling with my father in my fancy new dress at the Waldorf Astoria was not an experience that a young farm girl like me could have imagined. I remember wishing the day would last forever. I looked forward to reliving it again and again through conversations with my sister in the years to follow.

Chapter 20.

A Mountain Vacation

Nothing is more memorable than a smell. One scent can be unexpected, momentary, and fleeting, yet conjure up a childhood summer beside a lake in the mountains.

~Diane Ackerman, American poet, essayist, and naturalist

A rare overnight trip took us to the Adirondack Mountains. We set off early on a glorious summer morning, riding across the countryside, past farms and tiny villages, with the windows open and our hair blowing in the breeze. My siblings and I sat on pillows so we could enjoy the scenery. There were no carseats or seatbelts in those days. Soon, the car strained to climb steep roads that zigzagged through the heavily wooded range. Along the way, we passed logging trucks hauling their loads down the mountain to sawmills in the valley below.

Dad parked the car at a mountain overlook, so we could eat our picnic lunch while regarding the "sightly" view, as he called it. A cloudless sky allowed us to observe the landscape for miles in the distance. I was sure I could see the entire world through the windshield of our 1950 Nash Ambassador.

I had learned to sing "America the Beautiful" that year in the fourth grade. Now the lyrics, "purple mountain majesties," took on significance. The imposing Adirondacks dwarfed the rolling hills of our farmland. Tiny houses and barns dotted the valley, the livestock appearing no larger than insects. Some plowed and planted fields delineated neat little multi-colored squares and rectangles painted in yellows, browns, and greens.

We started to open the doors when Mom yelled, "Stay in the car!" Across the highway, she had spotted a giant black bear. He stood on his hind legs atop a large round boulder, stretching his front paws toward the sky as if he owned the wilderness. With the windows rolled up, we watched the furry giant amble away. We ate our sandwiches in the car and soon were on the move toward our overnight destination. One day and one night comprised the usual extent of our childhood vacations. Dad was always needed back on the farm.

Shortly after noon, we pulled into a gravel driveway edged by mature trees and colorful flowering shrubs, whose scent reminded me of grape soda. Not that I had much experience with soda. The only time I remember drinking it was when Marion and I stayed with our cousins, Kathleen, Deanna, and Audrey, who had moved off the farm to Walton, New York—a *real* town with sidewalks and stores. Marion and I spent a week with them one summer, and I remember walking to a nearby store where I bought a grape soda. What a treat! Since I wasn't allowed to have soda pop, I was determined to drink it before returning to their house. However, I hadn't realized that opening the glass bottle required a bottle opener. As we passed a stone wall, I smashed it, breaking off the neck, and guzzled it right there. Since I don't remember a trip to the ER, I assume I neither cut my hand nor swallowed any shards of glass.

A friendly older couple stepped off the porch of their double-wide trailer, greeted us warmly, and handed Dad the key to an inviting cabin on a nearby rise. It had a small front porch and steep back steps. Furnished with slip-covered furniture, the inside smelled faintly of fireplace ashes.

Behind the cabin, the expansive lawn sloped to a gleaming lake. Large shade trees surrounded the property, their branches swaying in the cool breeze and keeping the bugs at bay.

After unpacking the car, Mom set about making the beds, and Dad fished off the dock using earthworms as bait. He had dug them out of our garden at home and transported them in a Mason jar of moist dirt. Soon he caught several good-sized catfish, which he cleaned on a rock at the water's edge.

It didn't take long for us to change into our swimsuits. Mom riffled through the kitchen's knotty pine cabinets and drawers, where she discovered large spoons and measuring cups we could use to dig in the sand. Laughing and screeching with delight, four children raced toward the lake, where we were soon splashing in the icy water. Mostly, the shoreline was rocky, but we played happily all day in a small patch of sand with our makeshift shovels and pails.

Marion and I noticed a canoe approaching. To our amazement, a girl who appeared no older than Marion's eleven years steered it confidently across the lake. She had long dark hair and wore an orange life jacket. "Hi! My name's Amy," she called. "I live over there." She pointed toward the opposite shore. Marion waved and called back. I waved but said nothing, shocked that the girl's parents would let her go off alone in a canoe. I wondered what would happen if she got lost or the canoe flipped. What if she should meet a pirate or a sea monster?

"Wanna take a ride?" Amy called. "I have an extra life jacket." She paddled in circles to keep the canoe in one spot and seemed at ease maneuvering it wherever she wanted. She would swing the paddle from one side to the other, dipping it into the clear water, a bright glint of light flashing as the sun reflected off the wet surface.

"Hold on," answered Marion. "I'll ask." She ran up the hill to the cabin, taking the steep back steps two at a time, to ask Mom's permission. I already knew what the answer would be. Mom, who had never learned to swim, feared water. Marion usually argued and hassled with our mother's decisions, but I accepted them. Life

Dad and Kids on Back Steps of Cottage

was easier that way. Long before, I had decided to let my sister keep her title of "rebel." As I anticipated, Mom refused to let her go, resulting in some dramatic but short-lived sulking.

Later in the afternoon, I saw Amy again, paddling her canoe alone across the lake. I tried to imagine how it would feel to be allowed such an extreme degree of independence.

When Mom called us for supper, we were tired and famished from a day of energetic play. In an iron skillet bubbling with Crisco shortening, she had fried the flour-coated fish atop the gas range. We ate at a picnic table in the backyard. The fish smelled rich with pepper and fried flour and tasted even better, especially accompanied by the fresh, juicy sweet corn we had brought from home. Whenever I smell fish frying, my memory transports me to that picnic supper beside the pristine mountain lake.

That night, Marion and I slept on cots in the kitchen while our younger brothers shared the tiny cabin's only bedroom with our parents. The bright moon cast its light through a slit between the curtains.

Sometime after midnight, a frightening noise awakened me. The rattling seemed to shake my cot and came from the direction of the window over the kitchen sink. I convinced myself it was the black bear we had spotted on the mountain drive. It was trying to break into the cabin to eat my whole family. Soon the bear would break the glass and climb in. If I screamed, it would crash through the window and attack me. If I got out of bed, it would devour me before I could reach the safety of my parents.

I tried to wake Marion without provoking the bear's attention, but my sister was grinding her teeth—a familiar habit telling me she slept soundly. She didn't respond to my anxious whispers. Terrified to move or cry out, I hid under the patchwork quilt as if it would protect me and listened. Trepidation kept me awake and trembling for what seemed like hours. Finally, I could no longer fight my heavy eyelids and dozed off. The last thing I remember thinking was at least I would be asleep when the bear ripped into my flesh, tore me apart, and swallowed my body parts before devouring the rest of my family.

When morning came, I discovered I was alive and breathing with four intact limbs. Mom, who was scrambling eggs in an iron skillet, announced, "Come on, sleepyheads. Let's get going. We have a long drive ahead of us."

As I yawned and stretched, Dad entered the kitchen and crossed the linoleum floor toward the sink. The window was unbroken. Thankfully, the bear gave up and went away.

"After breakfast, I'll clean these and pack them in ice," Dad said to Mom. He pulled out a stringer of catfish that he had kept alive overnight in the sink. So, that's what had made the frightening noises that kept me awake. I was glad I had refrained from telling anyone about the vicious bear. I never would have heard the end of it.

Chapter 21

A Trip to the Big City

Being on top of the world doesn't mean anything unless you know how it feels at the bottom.

~Anonymous

When Marion and I were ten and eight, Mom took us to an allergy specialist in Syracuse. Accustomed to medical appointments, I felt excitement over the adventure rather than apprehension about the procedures. Mom had finally earned her driver's license, but I could tell she was nervous about driving and parking in a strange city. Once we reached the outskirts, her hands grabbed the wheel so tightly that her fingers turned white, and her eyes darted here and there as though she expected a sudden catastrophe.

The three of us planned and prepared for the trip days in advance, selecting our outfits carefully and deciding how we would style our hair. Mom splurged by buying a copy of the *Ladies Home Journal* at the grocery store. Worried about looking like country bumpkins, we studied pictures of movie stars in the magazine that cost less than fifty cents. Marion and I settled on matching dresses Mom had made the year before. We accessorized our outfits with ruffled socks and the patent leather shoes we usually saved for church. Mom even let us wear some of her makeup and jewelry, and we had fun pretending to be runway models.

Mom said we would eat lunch at Hotel Syracuse, the big fancy hotel on

Sisters Dressed as Twins

East Genesee Street. She told us it was famous for its swanky décor and elegant cuisine, but I wasn't sure what to expect. For months, Mom had been saving her bakery money to treat her girls to this rare indulgence.

"After lunch, we'll shop for school clothes," Mom said. This statement meant we would find a fabric store and pick out patterns and cloth for her to fashion into matching dresses for us. Although Marion and I were two years and two inches apart, onlookers often mistook us for twins because Mom insisted on dressing us alike. I didn't like being my sister's clone. It made me feel like I was not only the second child but second-best. I preferred my own identity, and I suspect Marion did, too.

The twenty-five-mile trip seemed to take forever, but we finally found the doctor's downtown office. The appointment took the whole morning, most of which we spent waiting to be examined, waiting for the nurse to inject us with allergens, waiting for the reactions, and waiting for the test results. Soon, my arms and back were covered with red bumps that itched madly, but Mom said I mustn't scratch them. Back in the waiting room, Marion and I sent each other into spasms of giggles when we pantomimed scratching our own and each other's arms. We called it "air-scratching." Trying to keep us from disturbing others, Mom pretended not to be amused, but we saw her struggling to control her own snickers amid our antics.

Finally, with our allergens identified, the specialist concocted a customized serum for each sister. Our own doctor in Fulton would administer the injections every other week. That might not sound like fun, but I took it in stride. I was used to getting shots and looked forward to life without the incessant asthma attacks and outbreaks of eczema that plagued my childhood.

In addition to allergy shots, the specialist recommended that Mom purchase a particular air-filtering gizmo for our bedroom window. We knew Dad would sigh and say it was "ridiculously expensive," but Mom would convince him it was for the best. She would argue that the initial purchase would save him money by decreasing future medical bills.

Finally, after the lengthy appointment, we headed for Hotel Syracuse. The building looked massive, causing me to wonder if we might get lost inside its impressive brick edifice. Its three towers loomed over us as we approached the front entrance guarded by grumpy-looking gargoyles. Once inside the foyer, I felt dwarfed by tall marble columns and a massive crystal chandelier. Fresh flowers and palm trees adorned the spacious lobby, and when I gazed upward, I saw mermaids painted on the domed ceiling. Mom approached the front desk, behind which a beautiful hand-painted mural covered the wall. The desk clerk informed her that there was more than one restaurant in the hotel and directed us to a small tearoom with lace curtains on the windows.

Our lunch experience was worth the wait. Other than the Waldorf Astoria in New York City, I had not seen such an elegant place except on television. As the tuxedoed steward led us to a table by the front window, I felt like a movie star on the red carpet. With gloved hands and a flourish, he laid cloth napkins across our laps.

A friendly formal-looking waiter served us hot tea from a china pot dressed in a floral cozy. Mother and daughters drank tea from dainty cups with tiny roses that coordinated with the pink tablecloth and napkins. Chances are it was the same brand of Lipton that we drank at home, but somehow it smelled and tasted exotic as we sipped from those delicate cups.

I wanted to order my favorite sandwich, egg salad, but because the allergy testing had revealed a sensitivity to eggs, Mom vetoed my choice. With my strong aversion to onions, I secretly wished the test had also indicated an allergy to them. I ordered tuna salad instead, risking it might contain onions, but I was too shy to ask.

To my delight, the tuna salad arrived onion-free. I liked how the thinly sliced white bread had been cut into triangles with the crusts trimmed off. It was one of my first exposures to store-bought bread. Soft and gooey, this bread tasted more like cake. Even in my school's cafeteria, the rolls were made from scratch daily, and Mom always made our bread at home. Her homemade bread was delicious, too, hot from the oven and paired with hand-churned butter, but the slices were thicker and the texture denser. I discovered I could roll the restaurant's bread into scrumptious dough balls with my tongue.

Next to the sandwich sat a crispy, green lettuce leaf adorned with vegetables artfully carved into rosettes. As much as I enjoyed fresh crisp carrots, celery and radishes, I hesitated to crunch them between my teeth and destroy the skillful artwork. I wasn't even sure they were edible.

Mom said we could share a dessert, so we settled on chocolate cake. When it arrived, the generous piece seemed large enough for our entire family to share. We split the rich, three-tiered confection smothered in thick chocolate icing. What a treat! Determined to act sophisticated, we restrained our outward pleasure, but undoubtedly some lip-smacking was involved. I wonder what the waiter thought when he saw the chocolate-stained napkins we left behind.

It was time to locate a fabric store. The waiter directed us to Chappell's, a locally famous family-owned department store based in Syracuse. We rode the elevator to the sewing department on the second floor. Sitting at an easel-like table, we leafed through stacks of Simplicity and McCall's patterns. I never saw so many pattern books, fabric bolts, or sewing notions. I wondered what it would be like to wear a store-bought dress like many of my school friends and wished I could try on the stylish ones we had passed on the first floor.

Finally, it was time to choose the cloth for our frocks. When Marion and I couldn't agree on the color or print, Mom let us select two different fabrics, a blue-and-white checked material for me and beige corduroy for my sister. But Mom stopped short of splurging on two patterns. She would make Marion's dress first, then cut the same pattern to fit me. She promised our dresses would be beautiful. They always were.

I could hardly wait to get home and tell my brothers about our adventure. I was sure they'd wish they had allergies, too.

Chapter 22.

My Forever Friend

A friend is one who knows you and loves you just the same.

~Elbert Hubbard, American writer, publisher, artist, and philosopher

When I met my forever friend, she was a sweet intelligent pretty girl named Linda. I was drawn to Linda because of her confident demeanor and witty humor. I wanted to feel and act confident, too, but I didn't know how. Although Linda and I lived a mere three miles apart—in the country, three miles is practically next door—we didn't meet until the fourth grade. We attended an elementary school in Mexico, while Palermo's country school was being rebuilt after the fire. Each morning the bus picked up Linda before me, and she always saved a seat for me. Since we were in different classrooms that year, our only opportunity to talk was during the long ride to and from school—long because it detoured on winding country roads through an isolated area that we later dubbed Appalachia.

Linda and I discovered we shared the same piano teacher, and our parents once attended school together in the one-room schoolhouse we knew as Palermo Elementary's bus garage. It was the beginning of a lifelong friendship.

Finally, Linda and I were together in the fifth grade, solidifying our relationship. We even developed our own secret sign language so we could talk to each other from across the classroom. That ended when Mr. Haynes, our heartthrob teacher, caught us in the act. His reprimand wasn't unkind, but Linda and I, both conscientious students, felt embarrassed and contrite about our silly behavior.

On Friday, Linda invited me to spend the night at her house. I was excited but nervous. It would be only my second sleepover, and I was anxious about meeting her parents and sister. I worried I'd say something stupid or insult someone without realizing it.

When Friday arrived, I rode the bus home with Linda and her older sister. As we pulled up to her house, Linda's father, who later became a Nazarene pastor, was watering a massive colorful flower bed in their front yard. Recently, Linda informed me that her father never returned home from work until after 5:00 pm. Evidently, my memory has combined numerous visits to her house that included Saturdays. Anyway, I remember that he turned off the hose and walked to the road to meet us with smiling eyes. Linda and her sister got big hugs, and their father offered me a friendly handshake. "Welcome, young lady," he said. "Let's go inside and see if there are any cookies waiting for us." I was stunned by this warm reception but could tell Linda took it in stride. Except for Mr. Haynes, I had seldom met a man who acknowledged children and showed genuine interest in them.

Though more reserved than her husband, Linda's mother smiled at us as we entered the house. I noticed she didn't hug her daughters, but she, too, greeted me congenially and asked about our day. She invited us to sit at the table in her ordinary but immaculate kitchen and help ourselves to the cookie jar. The slim petite neatly dressed woman poured generous glasses of milk from a glass bottle—I was too shy to tell her I couldn't drink milk, so I left it on the table. I noticed she walked with a limp. Later, I learned she suffered from painful arthritis.

I still hadn't spoken a word, but Linda's parents didn't let my shyness stop them from friendly banter. The blatant absence of criticism cynicism and melancholy was jolting. These parents spoke to their daughters like they were adults and valued the girls' opinions. Not that my parents weren't friendly, especially to visitors, but Dad was often opinionated, holding solid views that left little room for healthy debate, and Mom would go to great lengths to avoid discord. In Linda's home, my comfort level increased with every passing moment, and soon I entered the conversation with nods of "yes" or "no." It was the first of many treasured visits to this pleasant home.

Simply furnished, Linda's house was uncluttered and well-maintained. My house, in contrast, was messy. Mom overstuffed the limited closets leaving as many clothes hung outside the doors as inside, and she usually had more than one sewing project laid out in the dining room. Piles of mail, newspapers, and magazines overflowed the kitchen counters. Cabinets, dressers, and cupboards were jam-packed with stuff we needed and might need in the future. While my parents valued cleanliness both in their home and hygiene, they found it difficult to throw anything away.

Through comparison, I became more aware than ever that my family's tired old farmhouse required some severe purging and renovation. With four children, the atmosphere could be loud and chaotic. Linda's home was peaceful, neat, and sparkly clean.

Linda and Me at
Our High School Graduation
1967

Whenever I visited my friend, her sister retreated to her bedroom, emerging only for meals. Unlike Linda, who bubbled with personality, her sister was serious-natured and unapproachable. In all the years of my visits, I scarcely got to know her.

Although I had arrived on a Friday evening, Linda and I finished our homework before dinner. It was the rule at her house. After dinner, we played ping pong in the basement—an actual, finished basement, not a dark, scary cellar with a dirt floor. I had never played ping pong before and felt embarrassed by my lack of skill. The game didn't last long since I wasn't a worthy opponent. Next, we spent some time at the piano, playing duets. Again, I felt inept, recognizing my friend was far more accomplished than I. She could even play by ear, creating intricate arrangements of familiar hymns.

Before bedtime, Linda's family gathered in the living room for devotion time. Soon after kneeling for prayer, Linda and I suffered a sudden, uncontrollable attack of giggles precipitated by someone's expression of flatulence. The harder we tried to stop, the more we giggled. I was mortified by my lack of self-control, afraid of being scolded or, worse yet, asked to leave. I adored the geniality of this setting and longed for the same kind of structure and predictability in my world. I would like to have stayed there forever and would've been humiliated if asked to leave. Quickly, Linda's dad drew the prayer to a close and, with his characteristic twinkle, said, "Well, I guess it's time for tired girls to go to bed." He said it without rancor, judgment, or any hint of scolding.

Typically, my siblings and I spent Saturday mornings watching cartoons on the new black-and-white console television that had been added to our living room. We would sit on the floor in our pajamas with bowls of Wheaties, laughing at the antics of Donald Duck, Bugs Bunny, and that totally predictable Wile E. Coyote.

Linda's house had no television. At first, it struck me as odd, but I didn't miss it. Instead, I enjoyed the alternate activities that my clever friend produced effortlessly. After a breakfast of pancakes and bacon, we washed and dried the dishes, then played numerous games of *Concentration*, which Linda always won, followed by various board games like *Sorry!* and *Chinese Checkers*. After we played more piano duets, Linda invited me to take a bike ride. I had never ridden a bike, not even on the handlebars of Dad's bike. I was always afraid to try. Dad used his bicycle as transportation between the two farms. Sometimes Rodger or Mark rode on the handlebars, but I feared falling. I declined Linda's invitation, knowing that I would surely embarrass myself.

***

Eventually, I gathered enough courage to invite Linda to spend the night at my house. Several days before the nervously anticipated event, I cleaned the upstairs bedroom that I now shared with Marion. Reluctantly, my sister agreed to move out for the night but refused to help me tidy up. "She's your friend, not mine," she declared. While my sister was not particularly kind to me when we were children, we grew to be best friends.

I wondered how I'd convince Mom that our house was unacceptably messy without hurting her feelings. I gave up and simply started cleaning and tidying. I dusted the living room furniture, organized clutter, vacuumed the main level, and mopped the kitchen floor. "What's gotten into you?" Mom asked.

"I just felt like helping," I said. My ancient house with worn furniture would never sparkle like Linda's, but at least my efforts made it slightly more presentable.

Aware that Linda was unaccustomed to brothers, I hoped mine would be on their best behavior. I wondered if Marion would blast that awful rock 'n roll music she liked. I was convinced Linda's parents disapproved of rock 'n roll, and I grew more nervous by the minute that they would forbid our friendship.

When Friday arrived, Linda got off the bus at my house. As usual, Mom was working at her sewing machine in the dining room. She had covered the table with fabric pieces pinned to various pattern shapes. Scraps of fabric and bits of thread littered the floor, and half-sewn garments hung in the doorways, but

Linda didn't seem to notice the mess. She walked right up to Mom, side-stepping the ironing board, and said, "Hi, Mrs. Loomis" and "Thank you for inviting me" without a trace of shyness.

Five-year-old Mark had started setting up his *Lincoln Logs* when Rodger approached his log tower and kicked it over. Mark screamed and lit into Rodger. Soon they were rolling, yelling, wrestling, and punching each other. Typically, this scene played out many times, but I was hoping that day wouldn't be typical. I shuddered to have my friend witness such a spectacle, thinking she wouldn't want to visit again. Mom broke up the fight without resolving the underlying issue, a quarrel that may have started on the bus. Embarrassed, I wondered what Linda was thinking.

"Let's all go to the kitchen for a snack," Mom said. She had baked some of her delicious homemade bread. It was still warm from the oven when she cut thick slices and spread them with butter and strawberry jam. The snack was more than acceptable, giving me hope that Mom was trying to put her best foot forward. Maybe Linda wouldn't notice the counter, table, and kitchen sink were strewn with dirty mixing utensils and bread pans.

"Let's go upstairs," I suggested. The goal was to distract my friend from my household's general disorderliness, but Linda didn't appear to notice. She seemed comfortable during that first stay and her many subsequent visits. She even enjoyed playing with my rambunctious brothers. Many years later, we reminisced about our many visits to each other's homes. I told her I adored her house's pristine peaceful environment. She told me she enjoyed being with my family, finding richness in the cacophony of my household. She especially enjoyed "horsing around" with my brothers.

Our friendship took a hiatus when we left for different colleges, but when we renewed it several years later, it was like we had never separated. Currently, we live many states apart, seeing each other no more often than once a year, but our phone conversations last for hours. Although we each developed a wide range of friendships through the years, Linda remains my cherished forever friend.

Chapter 23.

Surviving the Cold War

The Cold War isn't thawing; it is burning with a deadly heat. Communism isn't sleeping; it is, as always, plotting, scheming, working, fighting.

~Richard M. Nixon, 37th president of the United States

At nine years old, I worried that an atomic bomb would explode without warning and separate me from my family. With the Cold War at its height, the threat of a nuclear attack hung over us menacingly. It was like living in the eye of a hurricane. It hadn't occurred to me that none of us would survive if my worst fear came to fruition.

My nightmares reflected the anxieties that consumed me during daylight hours. Walter Cronkite's nightly newscasts about the Soviet Union growing more powerful than the United States fueled my childish fears. Terms like "red scare," "super bomb," "iron curtain," and "arms race" permeated the news and seemed even more frightening on our new giant black-and-white television.

Mom prepared an emergency supply kit according to the radio announcer's instructions. Each monthly trip to the grocery store might include an extra can of Spam, a carton of powdered milk, or a jar of peanut butter. Mom filled hundreds of Mason jars with vegetables and fruits from the bountiful garden Dad planted every spring. The plot, spanning more than a half-acre, produced abundant yields of peas, sweet corn, string beans, tomatoes, squash, carrots, cabbage, and strawberries.

Tension mounted as preparations took shape for a family of six to hole up in our farmhouse's cramped dark cellar. We grew both fearful and excited. While Mom gathered supplies, my little brothers imagined armed combat with an unseen enemy, and Dad spent his few hours away from farm chores readying the cellar to become a bomb shelter. Growing up during the Great Depression had taught him that one's worst fears could come true and that careful preparation was the key to survival.

Dad built shelves beneath the basement stairs to hold a transistor radio, extra batteries, hurricane lamps, and safety matches stored in a glass jar. Canned goods lined one entire wall of the exposed stone foundation. On the opposite wall, long shelves held bins of blankets, quilts, and enough worn clean sheets and towels to open a bed-and-breakfast. On the dirt floor stood a small camp stove with a supply of Sterno cans and a metal box with essential tools and cooking utensils beside it.

I watched Mom fill gallon jugs with well water, adding a drop of bleach to each vessel to keep the liquid potable. She collected paper plates, cups, and other essential supplies and filled a box with puzzles, games, crayons, and coloring books she bought whenever they went on sale at the Woolworth in Fulton. I wished I could open the box and enjoy its forbidden activities instead of waiting for a catastrophic event.

Some nights, as Marion and I lay in bed, we talked about what it would be like to live in the dark cellar, subsisting on canned food and playing games until the danger passed. Not once did we question our parents' plan for survival or wonder how we would safely leave our shelter to use the bathroom upstairs or how we would prevent nuclear fallout from seeping through cracks in the stone foundation and around the cellar door.

World War II had ended just before we were born, but its horrors remained fresh in our parents' and grandparents' minds. As they discussed the Second World War, they forgot to reassure us that such an event probably wouldn't happen again and that this new Cold War surely wouldn't reach our shores. Perhaps they didn't know our school's *Weekly Readers* carried accounts of Nikita Khrushchev, portrayed as evil as Josef Stalin and Adolf Hitler.

Marion had just finished reading *The Diary of Anne Frank*. She was fond of regaling her impressionable younger sister with dramatic stories, true or imagined. I don't remember any specific tales, but I recall they were quite detailed and always held my interest. One night as we lay in bed, she shared the final installment of Anne Frank's diary, revealing the ultimate plight of Anne and her family. Of course, I burst into tears. That's when my sister had to quickly devise tactics–like scratching my back and promising to do some of my chores–

to reassure me before our parents heard the choking sobs and wanted to know what had caused my meltdown. Of course, Marion assured me, the ending would be different for *our* family. We would survive. "Yes," I averred. "I must survive!" I had an entire lifetime to live and countless goals to accomplish, including high school, college, marriage, children, a singing career, and a novel or two.

Writing had always invoked a powerful release of energy and emotion. In addition to music, writing was my salvation. I decided to keep a diary as Anne Frank had done. I imagined taking it to the cellar and recording my family's experience of surviving World War III. In its pages, I would express my deepest secrets and longings. I would record my poems, stories, and songs. One day, someone would find my journal and publish it for all the world to read...if there was to be a world beyond my childhood.

We participated in recurrent emergency drills at school, not the usual fire drills where classrooms emptied onto the front lawn and children gathered around the flagpole, waiting in silence until the all-clear alarm sounded. These exercises were different. Sometimes my classmates and I were instructed to crouch under our desks. Other times we spilled into the long tiled corridor from one end of the building to the other.

"Sit with your back against the wall and your knees bent. Put your head between your knees and cover your head with your arms," announced the principal over the loudspeaker. I wondered how this uncomfortable position could protect us from an atomic bomb explosion and how I would get home to my parents. Undoubtedly, the school's administrators had a plan. Adults always had a plan for keeping children safe. It was their sacred duty, after all. I obeyed and trusted.

Eventually, the drills lessened in frequency, finally disappearing altogether. Our family's cellar reverted to a place for storing firewood and garden plenty, and the urgency faded into memories of a strange and frightening era. Despite the overriding anxiety of my childhood, I finished grade school and graduated from high school and college. I married and raised two children. I fulfilled a long career in music education and music ministry and even became a published author. Repeatedly, the world's superpowers brought us to the brink of disaster, but, somehow, my family survived without living in the cellar.

Chapter 24.

Education with a Twist

I've learned that people will forget what you said, people will forget what you did, but people will never forget how you made them feel.

~Maya Angelou, one of America's most beloved authors and poets

From an early age, communicating with God felt as natural as breathing. I experienced a keen sense of my Creator's abiding presence. Perhaps this awareness came from regular attendance at church and Sunday school. Maybe it came from Mom's insistence that we recite The Lord's Prayer at the dinner table and before bedtime. Indeed, these rituals nurtured my faith practice, but my relationship with a powerful omnipresent loving higher power made the problematic parts of my childhood tolerable.

My tiny rural community offered religious education weekly during the school day. When I was in the fifth grade, children whose parents gave their permission were released to walk to the Grange hall around the corner from our newly rebuilt elementary school. For a fleeting moment, I wondered why some classmates stayed behind and what they did while I was gone. But I didn't dwell on the thought for long because that hour in the Grange hall soon became the highlight of my week.

Two rows of wood-slatted folding chairs arranged in an intimate semi-circle waited for us in the vast pine-paneled hall with the beamed ceiling and shiny wooden floor. The chairs faced a tall windowless wall. In front of the wall stood an easel covered with green felt. Two smiling women greeted us. With genuine enthusiasm, they arrived well-prepared to make Bible stories bubble forth like a mountain spring. I always chose a chair in the front row for the best view of their felt-backed visuals.

Immediately, we sat captivated by the Old Testament stories of David and Goliath, Noah's Ark, Abraham and Isaac, Miriam and Moses, and New Testament accounts of Jesus and His disciples. We sang songs, memorized Bible verses, and learned that God has always been and would always be—that God's love was unconditional. In that stark, often cold setting, I bathed in warmth from deep within and far beyond myself. It had nothing to do with the pot-bellied stove that struggled to heat the cavernous space. I can't recall how the women looked, whether young or middle-aged, or what they wore. Instead, I remember how they made me feel accepted, valued, intelligent, and loved by my Heavenly Father.

These principles stayed with me more than my childhood Sunday school lessons because the women's multimedia method accommodated each child's learning style, whether visual, auditory, or tactile. I didn't understand the wisdom of their approach until years later when I became a teacher. Often, the women brought objects for us to see and touch: an oil lamp from the Holy Land; colorful, hand-dyed fabrics; papyrus scrolls; or reproductions of famous religious art. They presented each story with an entire cast of felt-backed characters that they affixed to the easel at just the right point in the tale. They encouraged us to memorize scripture, rewarding our efforts with ceramic plaques and sculptures they had crafted, painted, and fired.

Memorization was never one of my strengths. Throughout my academic career, I always had to work diligently to retain information, especially if the subject matter didn't interest me. My mind wandered quickly, and my thoughts scattered like dandelion seeds in the wind. Even as a fifth grader, I knew memorizing one of the assigned passages would be difficult. But I couldn't forget that beautiful sculpture of Jesus sitting on a rock in his flowing robes, surrounded by awestruck children. With its vibrant blue, yellow, and red paint encased in shiny glaze, it would be the perfect addition to the desk in my bedroom. I noticed only three iterations of that scene, and I worried that other more competent children would claim them before I could.

The scripture I chose from the list was Isaiah 55:6–9. As I feared, memorizing it was a monumental task. I tried and tried to remember those words by reading, reciting, and copying them repeatedly. Every evening, after finishing my homework, I would practice. The first few verses might flow from my tongue, but soon my concentration waned; the next time I would have to sneak a peek to get started. I might get stumped by the simplest word or phrase. It wasn't the first time I thought I was stupid.

Arriving at the Grange hall the following week, I felt defeated, sure my recall would fail, convinced that *I* was a failure. Only twice had I been able to get through the entire passage without referring to the printed page.

Now two of the beautiful sculptures remained on the table before me. As one of the women presented the lesson, the other led individual children to a far corner of the room to hear their memory verses. I grew increasingly anxious. I simply wouldn't be satisfied with a plaque of the Ten Commandments or the sculpture of David Watching His Sheep, despite his colorful robe. No. I had my heart set on Jesus and the Children.

Finally, it was my turn. Tension mounted as I noticed only one sculpture on the table. Following the teacher to the appointed corner, my mind went blank. I knew I wouldn't be able to start the recitation. The figurine was lost to me. I sat facing my judge, fighting tears. After what seemed like an hour in my silent purgatory, the woman raised her eyebrows in anticipation and began, "Isaiah fifty-five...."

"Right," I said, staring at my hands. "Isaiah fifty-five, verses six through nine."

"Good. Go ahead," the teacher coaxed. Again, she waited. Again, I choked.

"Seek ye the Lord..." she started.

"...while he may be found."

"Yes. Call ye upon him..." my cheerleader continued.

"...while he is near." And so it went, with her prompting me to finish each sentence. I was sure she would withhold my reward. I didn't deserve it anyway. She would probably even scold me for not spending enough time on the assignment I had elected to accomplish. There was no requirement, after all. The exercise was voluntary.

She clasped her hands in her lap and smiled at me when we finished. "You did it," she said with a sigh. "I can tell you worked hard. Go to the table and pick out a prize."

I wanted to hug her, but I was too shy. I don't think I even said, "Thank you." I stood and walked toward the table where one statue remained. As I lifted it, claimed it, and cradled it, I didn't comprehend the enormity of the lesson I had learned that day. But I've thought about the moment many times since. It was an experience that changed my life. I had expected this teacher to shame me as I shamed myself for being less than perfect. Instead, I was granted unmerited grace by a true disciple of Jesus Christ, who patterned her words and actions after the Savior himself. No sermon has ever been as influential or uplifting as that woman's expression of perfect love, acceptance, and encouragement of a young girl who needed it desperately.

Bible study and public education seldom co-existed in the 1950s, except in the Catholic tradition. There were no Catholic churches in our area. At the time, I had no idea how unusual this weekly event was in a Protestant child's experience. When I thought to question my mother about the program, she was too old to remember how it came about. "I think they were missionaries," was her only explanation. Missionaries to an elementary school in Palermo, New York? Although something was missing from Mom's account, it didn't matter. It was the outcome that carried weight. My unique religious education blessed me for one hour each week during the fifth and sixth grades. More than illuminating my understanding of God, it taught me revelations about myself that I wouldn't recognize until much later in life. I learned that although God loved me exactly as I was, I held the potential to be more than the bashful insecure dim-witted girl I thought I was. I learned that as far back as 1600 BC, God chose imperfect humans like Moses and David to become influential leaders and accomplish God's purposes. While the Bible's myriad authors didn't necessarily write factually, I learned that they were inspired to write *truthfully* about spiritual responses within their limited understanding of scientific fact.

Still, I wish I knew who those women at the Grange were, where they came from, and how they managed to insert their selfless evocative agenda into my school days. I would like to thank them.

Chapter 25.

Family and Food

All sorrows are less with bread.

~Miguel de Cervantes, 16th-century Spanish author of Don Quixote

It was during the 1950s that my maternal grandparents operated a home bakery. Before dawn each weekday, Grandma Mansfield began mixing and baking dozens of cookies, loaves of bread, and yeasty dinner rolls. With three ovens, she had perfected her system of rotating the large trays of doughy goodness to ensure even browning. Whenever we visited, the aroma of baking bread greeted us as soon as we stepped through the farmhouse door into her bustling kitchen.

Tall for a woman and rather plain, Grandma had one false tooth held in place by a silver wire that shimmered in the light. When she laughed, her head flew back, and her high-pitched giggle exposed a girlish side of her nature that she rarely revealed to her grandchildren. Rather than hugs and praise, she spoke a love language of delicious baked goods.

A flour-covered bib apron covered one of her faded floral dresses, and a kerchief concealed her tightly permed hair. Support hose and sturdy shoes allowed her to stand in her kitchen for hours as sweat beaded her brow. But, setting aside her baker's uniform for Sunday services and other outings, Grandma donned her finest frock, with matching jewelry and pillbox hat, to assume her undisputed position as the family matriarch.

A fine dusting of sifted flour covered every surface of Grandma's kitchen: counters, table, butcher block, and floor. My siblings, cousins, and I found contentment in the inviting aromas of vanilla, molasses, ginger, and yeast that tickled our nostrils. She would offer each grandchild one cookie, either sugar or molasses, or one thick slice of warm bread with butter. Although her unique recipes produced soft, scrumptious cookies no less than six inches in circumference, I preferred the bread and butter. I would let the butter melt into the center until it sank with the weight of it, leaving a crispy crust around the edge. Folding the slice in half, I devoured every aromatic morsel as warm liquid dripped through my fingers and ran down my chin. Without supervision, I could have consumed a whole loaf by myself and gladly suffered the consequence of my gluttony.

Grandma Mansfield invented playdough long before the commercial brand was conceived. To occupy us while she carried out her tasks, she would hand each of us a gooey ball of bread dough to roll and knead and roll some more. She seated us around the kitchen table next to the window, each with a floured rectangle of wax paper, and encouraged us to form our dough into shapes.

My grandparents' dining room was central to their farmhouse with other rooms branching out like the points of a star. There, on the round pedestal table, Grandpa placed a metal machine that heated and sealed the edges of clear cellophane wrappers. Once the bread and cookies cooled sufficiently on wire racks, Grandma could begin the next stage of production. Wrapping each loaf in a sheet of cellophane, she ran it through the machine with its hot plates on either end of a conveyor belt. The heated cellophane crinkled as it adhered to itself, creating an airtight wrapper. To this day, when I smell the melting plastic of a laminating machine, it brings back the memory of that contraption on my grandparents' dining room table. When all the bread was packaged, she moved on to the dinner rolls and stacks of a dozen cookies each, her hands flying through their familiar routine. Once I was old enough, she sometimes allowed me to count and stack the items for each order and check them off a list. "Always double check," she warned. "We don't want to shortchange anyone."

In the living room beyond this makeshift factory, the black-and-white television was tuned to Grandma's favorite soap operas like *General Hospital,* so she could keep up with her "stories" as she packed the freshly baked products and added labels. While I found the TV distracting, she seemed capable of multitasking as she carried on conversations, supervised grandchildren, checked on final batches in the kitchen, and operated an efficient packing department.

Since Grandma and Grandpa lived in the country, their customers didn't stop by to retrieve their orders. Rather, Grandpa packed them in cardboard boxes and loaded them into Woody, his wood-paneled station wagon, for delivery to customers throughout the county. By the time I was old enough to be aware of their business, my grandparents had acquired an impressive following of loyal clients for miles around. They even supplied some of the grocery stores in the nearby towns of Fulton and Mexico.

Grandma finished the baking and wrapping by 2:00 pm each day and sent Grandpa off to make deliveries and collect payments while she cleaned the kitchen. It would take her delivery-boy husband until suppertime to complete his assignment because, being a friendly gregarious guy, he loved to stop and chat with each customer before moving on to the next.

It was time for Grandma to fill her deep kitchen sink with hot soapy water and wash the oversized metal bowls and myriad baking utensils, each covered in a glue-like substance. Next, she scrubbed every surface, including the floor, disinfecting them with nose-stinging bleach. I wondered how she could bring herself to annihilate the evocative aromas of vanilla, molasses, and spices.

Once a month on a Saturday, Grandpa drove into town with a list of ingredients to purchase in bulk. He returned with Woody filled with bags of flour, sugar, salt, and baking powder, along with blocks of yeast, large cans of Crisco and molasses, and dozens of eggs. He would pull the car close to the kitchen door, open the tailgate, and swing one bag at a time onto his shoulder, then haul it to the large storage room behind the kitchen.

My grandfather was a jolly round bald man who smoked cherry-scented cigars...but never inside the house. Grandma would not allow tobacco odor to permeate her doughs and batters. Once each cigar diminished sufficiently, Grandpa extinguished it and chewed on the stub for hours. Watching it bob up and down between his lips like a harbor buoy, I wondered why it didn't jump out of his mouth as he talked.

I don't remember playing with toys at Grandma and Grandpa's house. Rather, we were expected to devise our own means of entertainment with games like hide-and-seek or tag.

Each summer, we carried metal pails to the wooded area behind the house to pick wild blueberries. The task of filling our buckets with berries the size of BBs required perseverance, especially since we consumed as many of the sweet, succulent nuggets as we harvested—maybe more. With our clothes, lips, and tongues stained blue, we presented our yield in anticipation of Grandma's juicy pies or cobblers with tender crusts that melted on the tongue. She did not offer these baked treats for sale. Rather, she reserved them for family gatherings.

Beyond the blueberry patch, a knoll provided a sledding hill just steep enough for young children to manage. In the winter, after a fresh snowfall, Grandma turned her large metal baking trays into makeshift sleds for us. Coating the bottoms with cooking oil helped them slip easily down the snowy incline. She and Mom would stand at the crest to clap and cheer us on. Dressed in snowsuits and faux fur-lined boots, we would slide down the hill and trudge to the top again and again until cold cheeks and rubbery legs forced us inside for hot chocolate and—you guessed it—homemade bread.

All these years later, I, too, am a grandmother. I don't bake bread or even cookies, but I'll never forget the weight and smell of a loaf of Grandma's bread, and I cherish her recipes for soft, scrumptious cookies. Through the years, I've tried to replicate them, but mine have never turned out as mouth-watering and aromatic as hers.

***

We spent every Thanksgiving Day at Grandma and Grandpa's house. All the maternal aunts, uncles, and cousins came for dinner, each of the women contributing whatever delicacy was her culinary specialty. Mom brought the pumpkin pies, my favorite. Sometimes she made them out of butternut squash and laughed when no one could tell the difference. I enjoyed helping in the kitchen, but with so many women vying for space, I just got in the way. It became my job to help my sister set the tables: the big round pedestal table in the center of the dining room and the kids' tables squeezed into the corners. Grandma always roasted two turkeys, a formidable task unless your kitchen boasted three ovens.

Each family gathering made for a full house. Mom had two brothers and a sister who all came with their families. Along with Mom's four children, her older brother Harold had seven; her brother Nick had two; and the youngest, Midge, had three. Usually, babies napped in the bedrooms, despite only curtains separating them from the other rooms. Underfoot toddlers climbed on chairs, dressers, footstools, anywhere they shouldn't. The men and older boys gathered in the living room to watch football games while the younger children reacquainted with cousins they saw only once or twice a year. We arranged card games or puzzles on the living room floor where we played amid the laughing and cheering of enthusiastic football fans.

Finally, Mom and the aunts called the children to sit in folding chairs around the card tables borrowed from our grandparents' church. Grandpa, seated at the giant round dining table, offered the blessing. Wherever Grandpa sat became the head. I remember wondering, year after year, how old I'd have to be before I could sit at the grown-up's table with its white lace tablecloth set with Grandma's finest china and stemware.

While Grandpa carved the first turkey, the women brought steaming platters and bowls from the kitchen, each piled high with traditional Thanksgiving fare that filled the whole house with tempting aromas. Soon the tables held an abundance of sumptuous food: roast turkey and stuffing, mashed potatoes with gravy, sweet potato casserole topped with melted marshmallows, canned peas and sweet corn from someone's summer garden, orange gelatin infused with raw, shredded carrots and celery, and homemade cranberry sauce. Everyone agreed that, on this occasion, overeating was acceptable, even expected.

After dessert, the children were excused to play outside while the adults loosened their belts and remained at the table to talk. It always snowed, at least a little, on Thanksgiving Day, but that didn't stop Marion and me from joining our girl cousins for our traditional walk-and-talk up the road. The country road where my grandparents lived, was lightly traveled on ordinary days, but on holiday afternoons, we might never see a car. The older girls talked about their respective schools, teachers, and friends, plus the latest hair styles, clothes, boyfriends, movie heartthrobs, and how soon they would be earning their driving permits. As the youngest cousin for many years, I seldom contributed to the conversation but instead listened intently, committing to memory every hint about how to be an acceptable teenage girl.

After a nice long stroll to counteract the tryptophan in our distended stomachs, we piled into one of our parents' cars parked in the driveway and pretended to be adult ladies driving and chatting about what we perceived as adult issues. I don't recall any specific conversations, but I'm sure we parroted topics discussed inside the house. I do remember thinking my cousins had much more interesting lives, especially Susan who attended school in town and whose friends and experiences were far more sophisticated than Marion's or mine. Her mom even had a maid.

Usually Cousin Susan became the first "driver" since the game was her idea in the first place. I worried we'd get in trouble for playing in the parked cars, but no one seemed to care, and no one stopped us. Staying in character, Susan would light a make-believe cigarette and, looking behind her, pretend to back out of the driveway. Whether there was a car parked behind ours was of no consequence. She proceeded to talk about her "children" and the challenges a "mother" faced in keeping her house clean and orderly. Marion and Judy—who were older, but less urbane than Susan—offered sage advice from their vast parenting experience as Susan turned the steering wheel from side to side. Occasionally, she used the turn signal, indicating she was about to make a pretend-turn to the right or left. Whoever rode shotgun was then obligated to lean one way or the other. Since it was usually snowing outside in November, Susan engaged the windshield wipers from time to time. Thump, thump, thump. And so, the game went until one of the other girls indicated it was time for her to relinquish the driver's seat. I wondered when I would get a turn to be the driver. I don't think I ever did.

I clearly remember Grandpa's funeral because it was my first exposure to a service with full military honors. I was in middle school when he suffered a heart attack in his sixties. The twenty-one-gun salute with its powerful finality filled me with terror. But it was the lone soldier's rendition of "Taps" that brought me to tears.

Grandma lived for another twenty years as a widow, closing the bakery and moving in with her daughter, Aunt Midge. That's when she began making customized Christmas gifts for every member of her extensive family. Each December 26th, she would start sewing, knitting, or crocheting in preparation for the following Christmas. Grandma has been gone for many years, but my husband and I still have the tree skirt she knitted for our first Christmas as a married couple.

On her deathbed, Grandma apologized to me for letting me play with eggshells in her kitchen sink when I was two. My allergy to eggs had not yet been diagnosed, and my hands and arms broke out in a nasty rash. Of course, I had no memory of the incident, but now, as a mother and grandmother, myself, I can relate to her need for confession and reconciliation before it's too late.

My Maternal Grandparents Nicholas and Marion Mansfield

Chapter 26.

Marion's Chicken Project

'There now,' she said with some satisfaction and, taking careful aim, she shut her eyes and chopped hard. It worked—but Marty was totally unprepared for the next event. A wildly flopping chicken—with no head—covered her unmercifully with spattered blood. 'Stop thet! Stop thet!' she screamed. 'Yer s'pose to be dead, ya—ya dumb headless thing.'

~Janette Oke, from her novel, *Love Comes Softly*

My sister decided to make some money by raising chickens, also known as broilers. These chickens could not look forward to a future of egg production. Instead, their life's purpose was to grow fat enough to be butchered and sold for meat.

Our parents warned Marion not to get attached to her cash crop, but when those adorable, fuzzy chicks arrived, it was hard for her to view them as commodities. They followed her around like little ducklings trailing behind their mama. I don't remember how many chicks there were or how many survived to adulthood, but I recall that Marion ended up with a significant flock. She was already counting her profit and her chickens before...well, you know how the saying goes.

Fortunately, the lovable-chick stage didn't last long, and soon they grew into not-so-cute chicken-feed guzzlers who toddled around the backyard pecking at the ground and clucking their unappealing ditties. As I recall, this process of maturation took one entire summer.

Finally, it was time. You would think that farm girls might naturally be familiar with poultry slaughtering, but we lived on a dairy farm. We didn't have a clue how to butcher a chicken. The only animals we slaughtered were pesky mice who helped themselves to the grain bins and silage. That process involved simply taking a pitchfork and squashing or impaling the nasty beasts without any emotional aftermath.

I don't remember how or why Aunt Midge, Mom's sister, got involved in this project, but I suspect Mom conscripted her for the job because Mom had her hands full raising four children in a house with few conveniences, while operating a bakery from her kitchen. Dad was otherwise engaged with farm duties. Perhaps it was because Aunt Midge liked to fish and had no problem gutting and cleaning the fish she caught. I suppose her lack of squeamishness qualified her for the job. Of course, Marion was expected to help by grabbing the scrappy belligerent creatures and carrying them to the guillotine. It was her project, after all.

Earlier, Dad had retrieved a fat tree stump from the woodpile and set it in the backyard as a chopping block. Aunt Midge sharpened a hatchet and went to work beheading one hapless victim after the other. A bloodbath forced me into the house, and I was forever traumatized by the scene. The worst part was when a bloody, headless chicken scurried about the yard for several minutes before succumbing to its ultimate plight. It might seem like a laughable sight, but it was no laughing matter for this ten-year-old innocent.

With the gruesome deed accomplished, Mom put the little ones down for their afternoon naps, and the four of us "women" got busy with the next repugnant steps of feather-plucking, gut-purging, and carcass-washing in the kitchen sink. Then, Mom packed each broiler in a plastic bag and secured it with string.

If memory serves, Marion's customer list came from Mom's bakery clientele. Since some customers ordered multiple chickens, Mom had saved paper grocery bags for those larger orders.

Next, the meat must be delivered quickly while fresh. Aunt Midge also volunteered for that duty. My sister could hardly wait to rake in her proceeds and become independently wealthy at twelve. So, as Aunt Midge drove to each customer's house, Marion got out, delivered the order, and collected payment.

Later, Aunt Midge brought Marion home, offering to dispense the one remaining order of multiple broilers on her way home. Quickly, she retrieved her baby and toddler from Mom's care and headed for home. As promised, she stopped at the final customer's house, grabbed the grocery bag of chickens from the trunk, delivered them, and rushed home to start supper.

According to Aunt Midge, she tucked her children in bed after supper and prepared to wash a load of laundry. Disposable diapers didn't exist in those days, and it behooved any practical mother to wash the soiled cloth versions as soon as possible. She carried the bag to the laundry sink and dumped the contents, but, instead of diapers, two plucked headless chickens fell out.

Aunt Midge left her sleeping children with her husband, jumped in the car, and returned to the customer's house to make the exchange. She reported that they had a good laugh over the error.

After that one summer, Marion abandoned chicken farming as a means of becoming independently wealthy.

Chapter 27.

Stirring, Stirring, Stirring the Pot

You can't buy happiness, but you can buy ice cream. And that's kind of the same thing.

~ Anonymous

When I was a child, my favorite church activity, besides singing, was the annual ice cream social. Every July, Mom and Dad joined the other members of our tiny Methodist congregation to organize this significant fund-raiser. Its purpose was to help with the high cost of heating the church building during the long cold months that characterized Central New York's winters.

Since we lived on a dairy farm, my family's contribution to the event was a large can of fresh creamy cow's milk. Other members contributed sugar, eggs, flavorings, and rock salt. Leading up to the social, every rural homemaker accumulated ice from trays they had filled repeatedly, storing it in their freezers until needed, and anyone who owned an ice cream churn committed to lending it for the day. The only grocery store within eight miles of our little borough, provided hot dogs, hamburgers, and buns for the occasion.

For weeks, the event was publicized in church bulletins and area newspapers. Families came from every corner of Oswego County and beyond for a simple affordable meal topped off with scrumptious homemade ice cream.

When the day finally arrived, excitement filled our little farming community. Because television had only recently begun to replace the radio and had yet to dominate rural homes, churches served as more than places of worship. Our church was central to our lives, providing not only Sunday services and Christian education, but also opportunities for socialization and entertainment.

On ice cream social day, teenagers supervised and entertained the youngest children, freeing their mothers to spend a whole day in the church's kitchen. I wanted to be part of the action and looked forward to the day I would be old enough to help with preparations.

Finally, when I turned twelve, Mom pronounced me ready to assist. The kitchen was filled with apron-clad women bustling about and chattering happily. They assigned me to stir the rich custard comprised of eggs, cream, sugar, and corn starch until it thickened. Mom covered my hair with a colorful scarf, explaining that no one would want to eat hairy ice cream. She directed me to wash my hands with soap and warm water. Then, she tied a woman-sized apron around my waist, rolling the top to keep it from dragging.

The massive kettles were so deep I had to stand on a chair at the commercial-size range. "Make sure you don't get near the burner," Mom warned, "and stand with your legs apart for balance." With a long, wooden spoon in each hand, I stirred and stirred and stirred, first one direction, then the other, until my tiny arms felt as heavy as bricks and my shoulders ached from the effort. Although it wasn't as much fun as I had anticipated, my job provided satisfaction and, more importantly, the opportunity to eavesdrop on adult conversations.

Soon I discovered that my position as "official stirrer" carried great responsibility. "Take care not to let the mixtures come to a boil," Mom warned. She wasn't the only one to issue orders.

"Don't let the spoons scrape the bottoms of the pots," said someone else. "Scorching might have turned the custard brown."

"Stir constantly and evenly to prevent lumps," another woman directed. Sometimes Mom and the others would give me a break to rest my weary muscles, but I was determined to accomplish the task.

Over a double boiler, one woman melted generous, sixteen-ounce bars of semi-sweet chocolate and poured the shiny brown goodness into one kettle. Someone else emptied a whole bottle of pure vanilla extract—real vanilla, not the imitation stuff—into the other pot. With the flavorings added, intoxicating aromas tickled my nose. I swirled the dark and light mixtures together, watching as the marbled pattern transformed into smooth rich chocolaty pudding. At last, with pride and exhaustion, I announced that thickening had occurred.

Before the creamy liquids would be ready for the next step, they must cool to room temperature. Mom turned off the heat and covered the pots with clean dish towels to prevent a layer of scum from forming on top and keep black flies from diving into the alluring pools of elixir. I'm reminded of the horrid, sticky flypaper strips that hung from the ceiling of every farmhouse in the area. Although black flies were a nuisance, I found the flypaper covered with dead or dying flies more repulsive than the pests.

Soon it was time for the men to take over, packing ice and rock salt around the churns. As the women ladled cooled custard into metal cylinders, the men drew their chairs in a circle like a football team's huddle. With no electric churns in those days, they turned and turned and turned the cranks. The lengthy process allowed enough time to engage in conversations ranging from "which crops should bring the best harvest?" to "will the Yankees win the pennant this year?" I noticed that my often-melancholy father was cheerful and animated during this ritual. He enjoyed nothing more than sharing banter with his fellow farmers in the community, most of whom he had known his entire life.

By dusk, a long line of country folk from every corner of Oswego County spilled into the church's social hall, where tables covered with red-and-white checked tablecloths beckoned them to sit in wooden folding chairs and catch up on the latest gossip. My sister and I helped Mom and the other women cook hamburgers and hotdogs in an already over-heated kitchen. Then, forming an efficient assembly line, we served them along with homemade potato and macaroni salads contributed from the women's kitchens. We topped off each meal with a bowl of frozen goodness.

I could scarcely wait for my first taste of the luscious concoctions I had helped prepare. However, wait, I must. Once we had served all the customers, there was still plenty of work. Soon, Dad and the other farmers left for their evening farm chores. With the younger children now underfoot, darting about the social hall, we began the clean-up process: sweeping and mopping the floor, washing, drying, and storing pots and utensils, scrubbing grills, gathering and disposing of trash, and restoring order to the kitchen and dining hall.

I'm convinced the saying, "many hands make light work," originated with my church's ice cream socials. Each volunteer seemed to know what to do. With the tasks divided among us, it was still daylight when we finally served ourselves, gathering at one of the long tables to enjoy bowls of creamy homemade ice cream. That first taste was always worth the wait.

The ice cream social was one time I chose to ignore the stomach distress that would inevitably follow.

Chapter 28.

My Inspiration Garden

If you have a garden and a library, you have everything you need.

~Cicero, one of Rome's greatest orators and philosophers who
served as a Roman statesman in 63 B.C.

I will never forget a small framed print hanging on Grandma Loomis' bedroom
wall. The original watercolor may or may not have been famous. I never
noticed the artist's name. It was inconsequential when I was a child. But, after
all these years, my mind's eye can still gaze upon the scene as clearly as my child's
eyes once did.

The painting depicted an old English cottage surrounded by a low stone wall.
Unlike a formal English garden with tidy boxwood hedges, manicured lawns,
and neatly trimmed walkways, this parcel was messy, crowded, and exquisitely
beautiful. It looked like the gardener had tripped while carrying his load of seeds,
spreading them in wild, chaotic non-patterns. The captivating scene beckoned me
to swing open the wooden gate and enter a Victorian garden where summer roses,
cheerful daisies, and pink hollyhocks, vying for space, spilled over the cobblestone
walkway.

At either end of the cottage's thatched roof, swirls of smoke stretched upward
from robust stone chimneys to mingle with the billowy clouds above. A trellis of
climbing ivy surrounded the home's sturdy wooden door, and deep-set windows

with black shutters and mullions invited me to press my nose against the wavy panes.

As I nestled among Grandma's pillows, I appointed myself the official landscape architect of all that lay hidden behind the cottage. Following the stone footpath around the corner and through a vine-covered pergola, I entered the backyard where intricately arranged flowerbeds bordered a curvy patch of verdant lawn. Here the trail meandered among generous clusters of blooms, separating them according to genus and species. Flitting butterflies, hummingbirds, and honeybees devised their paths, disregarding local air traffic regulations.

Willow trees reached their weeping arms over the stone fortress far enough to offer privacy but not so much as to shade the flowers from life-giving sunlight. Behind them, along the wall's edge, neatly pruned shrubs of holly, laurel, and euonymus stood like sentries, guarding the vibrant annuals and perennials. Selected to bloom all summer and into autumn, these beauties emitted sweet intoxicating scents. Roses, gardenias, jasmine, and peonies competed for first place in my olfactory contest but kindly held their pollen on the canvas.

Beside a small pond, where lily pads floated and frogs performed their nightly choruses, I positioned an ornate wrought iron table painted white. Two matching chairs, their seats softened by thick floral cushions, completed the grouping shaded by low-hanging branches from the only tree permitted within the garden wall.

As a child, I made no effort to lock the painting in my mind's eye. I was barely conscious of its effect on me then. Yet it sparked my imagination and still does. Even now, when writer's block threatens, the cottage's rear garden is where I set up my laptop and invite my muse to join me for a cup of Earl Grey.

Chapter 29.

Moving On

Nobody can go back and start a new beginning, but anyone can start today and make a new ending.

~Maria Robinson, author of numerous child development books

I could include many other childhood memories in my memoir, but recall would be sketchy. I'll touch on a few here and allow the readers' imaginations to complete the stories.

One time, my siblings and I decided to climb onto the cows' backs and ride them like horses as they waited outside the barn for their evening milking. It had rained that day, and the barnyard was covered with a six-inch layer of mud mixed with manure. With no saddles to keep us astride our bovine broad-backed mounts, we ended up sliding off and wallowing in barnyard muck. Although my memory is not clear about the end of this adventure, I recall that it included some unpleasant hosing down with icy water before we could go home to take real baths.

I remember an incident when Marion was relatively young–maybe seven. She was swinging in our grandparents' backyard when she leaned back so far that her head caught on the ground, seriously twisting her neck. I feared it would paralyze her for life. From our parents' panic-stricken responses, I discerned that they did, too, which is likely where I got the idea. My sister spent the afternoon resting with an icepack on her neck but made a full recovery.

At one point, probably before Mark was born, there was a chubby dark-haired foster child named Keith. The only specific memory I have of him is when he stood on a chair, tipped backward, and smashed his fingers.

Once, a tractor-trailer failed to maneuver the curve in front of Grandpa's farm, crashed into a pasture, then flipped and burst into flames. According to Dad's animated report, he was inside the barn when he heard the crash, ran down the driveway, and crossed the road. When he found the unconscious driver still in the overturned cab, he rushed to the man's aid, pulling him out through the open window. As he grabbed the man's arm, his burned skin peeled off in Dad's hands.

Then, there was the pig that no one remembers but me. I have a clear memory of this creature being penned behind our barn near the rhubarb patch. I recall carrying buckets of food scraps from the kitchen and dumping them into the pen. Since the pig was not named, I always assumed it became a winter's-worth of dinners. But my siblings insist the pig is pure fantasy–perhaps I dreamed it. I will never know for sure.

I could write more about how isolation from my father and siblings affected me. I could include additional instances when I needed more emotional support from my parents. But thanks to God and this project, I've moved on. For me, the process of revisiting uncomfortable memories from childhood and addressing them from an adult perspective has diffused their intensity. Ultimately, the practice of detaching with acceptance and forgiveness frees me to remember my childhood's more positive, even humorous, aspects.

I've learned that no matter how hard we try to bury or deny unpleasant sensations surrounding our memories, we all are products of our upbringing as much as our parents were of theirs.

Years of journal entries prepared me for writing this book, revealing that–regardless of the contentment we find later in life–our childhood experiences invariably influence adulthood. We have no choice in what occurred, but we need not spend our adult lives as prisoners of the past. Through writing, I finally arrived at a healthy emotional place that includes understanding what made my parents and grandparents tick and how my childhood environment affected me.

Now, I can look forward with peace and joy to whatever years remain and focus on creating new memories with my children and grandchildren. As I approach my octogenarian decade, I'd say it's time.

From My Window

Pink-tinged clouds dance among the treetops,
fading to white as daylight dawns.
Beyond the mullioned panes,
a feathered warbler chirps its cheerful greeting.
Orange leaves tumble silently to earth,
swirling like so many helicopter blades.
Soon the trees will bare their weathered arms
in preparation for winter sleep.

In the autumn of life,
I bare my weathered arms toward God,
releasing regret, embracing forgiveness,
reaching ever closer to eternity
with the Savior, who has answered every prayer—
sometimes "Yes" sometimes "No" sometimes "Wait,"
always "Trust."

Throughout the seasons of earthly life,
God speaks to those who stop and listen,
"Peace be with you, my child. Go forth into this new day,
walking in My light, dwelling in My love."
I close my eyes and inhale Spirit's sweet breath.

Appendix

Memories from My Siblings

My three siblings' childhood experiences on the farm were quite different from mine and more positive. Because I was often isolated from my brothers, Rodger and Mark, it's as if we grew up in separate settings. I spent more time with my sister, Marion. Still, her experiences–and perceptions of those experiences–vary significantly from mine. I cannot discount or refute my siblings' interpretations, for I believe and respect their truth. Some of my childhood perspectives have surprised them, but thankfully, they also respect *my* truth.

I asked each of them to share a remembrance from their early years on the farm.

Mark, on His Third Birthday
and Rodger, Age 6

A Memory from Mark

Runaway Tractor

Most kids grow up playing in their backyard or at the park. But for dairy farm kids, the whole farm is their playground!

~Jordan Manning, agriculture blogger

From the time I started going to the barn with Dad, I wanted to be a farmer like him. My dream was to one day run the farm with my father. I assumed it would be in our family for many generations. So, after Grandpa's death, I was heartbroken when Grandma sold her half of the property, including the cows and farm equipment.

When I was about six years old, I was riding on the tractor with Dad, as I often did. We had just started off from the barn when Grandpa waved us down. Dad stopped and jumped off to talk to Grandpa, leaving the tractor running. I was always curious about what made things work, especially machines. So, I began playing with the various levers. Suddenly, the tractor was in gear, and away it went with me in the driver's seat. I don't remember feeling afraid. I simply grabbed the steering wheel and held on.

Rodger and Mark Harvesting Corn

When Dad realized what was happening, he ran to catch up and climbed up behind me. Lifting me quickly onto his lap, he slid under me onto the metal seat. He managed to reach the clutch and brake pedals before I destroyed any crops, leveled any fences, or injured myself. After pulling the tractor to a stop, Dad's only comment was, "I guess it's time to teach you how to drive a tractor."

Memories from Rodger

The Blessings of June

It is the sweet, simple things of life which are the real ones after all.

~Laura Ingalls Wilder, American writer known for the Little House on the Prairie series of books

Not only was I lucky enough to grow up on a farm, but I was also blessed with a June birthday. June in New York State is strawberry season! My mother claimed my love of strawberries owed to her overeating them before I was born and when I was a nursing baby. So, every June I still celebrate by eating as many strawberries as possible.

My most memorable birthday was my fifth for two other reasons. My hero then was Claude Rice. He owned a big diesel tractor, harvested our corn, and had been a cowboy sometime in his past. He was working on our farm on my fifth birthday, which meant we all had dinner together at midday. After dinner, he told me to go to the back of the house, where I found a brand-new toy farm set up on a low table. My hero, a new farm set, and strawberries! What a day!

My Brother

If thy brother wrongs thee, remember not so much his wrongdoing but more than ever that he is thy brother.

~Epictetus, Greek Stoic philosopher

Mark and I grew up so close that I was fifty before realizing he was three years younger. We did everything together. If I learned to drive a horse team at six, he learned at three. When we got the Allis Chalmers W-D 45, it didn't have power steering, power shift, or power brakes. We learned that if we combined our efforts, we could drive it. He would steer while I lay on my back, hanging from the steering column. By using both feet and my entire body, I could push in the clutch. Mark would then select the gear, and off we went. To steer, we would pull together with all our strength. This way, we learned to help on the farm.

When we wanted to harness the team, we would grab a horse collar and carry it to the stall. Mark would push it up to the elevated manger where I was standing, and I would take it the rest of the way. Similarly, we learned we could drag each harness up on the back of the big animals. I never heard Dad or Grandpa say, "Don't do that," or "You can't do that," or "You are too young," or "You aren't strong enough." Never, not once. We have pictures of Mark, at five years old, walking behind a team pulling a spring tooth harrow. Dad was close by supervising but was willing to allow the risk to help us grow into confident, valuable additions to the farm.

By the time Mark was six or seven, and I was nine or ten, Dad allowed us to operate a tractor hay bailer, pulling a wagon up and down the steep hills. The rig was at least sixty feet long and weighed ten tons. It was not uncommon for the whole thing to jack-knife and threaten to slide into a heap at the bottom of the hill.

One day I was raking hay on a particularly steep hill. Each time I went up the hill, the front of the tractor would raise up as if it might tip over backward. When I mentioned it to Dad at lunch, he simply picked up a concrete highway safety post that weighed a few hundred pounds and wired it to the front of the tractor with baling wire (the duct tape of farmers). I resumed my raking. He could have said, "That's too dangerous; I'll do it." But instead, he made me feel like he respected me enough to finish the job.

Dad's Bicycle

Nothing compares to the simple pleasure of riding a bike.

~John F. Kennedy, 35th president of the United States

When we were little, Dad didn't have a car, and we lived about a quarter mile up the road from the farm. Dad would put me in the front basket of his bike, and we would ride in the dark to do the morning chores. I remember it felt very cold, but it was probably summertime.

After a hard day that started at five a.m., he would pedal his bike and me uphill back home. That same bike was what I learned to ride. By wrapping a burlap bag around the crossbar, I would lean it up against the porch at the top of the hill and coast—I could not reach the pedals—downhill toward the garage, attempting to turn before reaching the road. The first dozen attempts were painful, but I eventually got the hang of it. Dad never tried to stop me, although I am sure the many crashes didn't do any good to his primary mode of transportation.

Years later, I saved twenty-five dollars and bought a used English-style bike which I proceeded to motorize. Dad drove me to the town of Mexico, where I had made a deal to buy a gas engine, and he let me take the cover off his tractor battery box to mount it. He never tried to show me the error of my ways but let me experiment and learn the hard way.

Horsepower

Farming looks mighty easy when your plow is a pencil and you're a thousand miles from the cornfield.

~Dwight D. Eisenhower, 34th president of the United States

Even though we grew up in the 1950s, the Loomis children had the opportunity to live in the early 1900s. We did everything with horses, from spreading manure to cultivating corn, also pulling the hay wagon and the oat mower/binder. Grandpa believed in horsepower, actual horsepower. We had a tractor, an Allis Chalmers W-D 45, which Dad used to bale hay, but I only saw Grandpa on the tractor once. That was because Dad had taken a vacation, the first time I saw him take a day off. We didn't use the word vacation in those days.

Mom and Dad took my sisters to New York City to attend a wedding. Whatever experiences they had could not possibly have been better than helping Grandpa run the farm at age six. Besides, when they returned home, I received a copper statue of a horse from the Empire State Building. What more could a boy ask for? That was the only time I remember Grandma working in the barn; even then, she wore a dress. I'm sure Grandpa didn't consider me an adequate replacement for Dad, although he would never overtly show any such attitude toward me.

A Memory from Marion

Grandma's Legacy

Grandmothers are voices of the past and role models of the present. Grandmothers open the doors to the future.

~Helen Ketchum, host of "Transitions," a public-access television show that examined senior life.

The weather in Central New York was always a topic of conversation. The cloudy days and seemingly endless winters placed a melancholy mood on everyone, and spring couldn't come soon enough. My siblings and I looked forward to our spring break from school, but since it was scheduled around Easter, it could occur any time from mid-March to late April. As kids who loved to play outdoors, we hoped for sunshine and warmth, but often winter lingered, and summer seemed a long way off.

I recall one favorite spring break in late April that was unusually warm. I was probably ten with my three tag-along siblings, eight, six, and three years old. We had great imaginations and could always find the raw materials for any activity, from pretend hunting or cowboys and Indians (as we had seen in TV Westerns) to playing house or school. We especially loved to play in the woods behind Grandpa's barn. There were trees to climb, critters to hunt with our "guns," rocks to make into forts, and just the simple appreciation of nature bursting forth all around us. There was also a clear, little stream where we would try to cool our burning faces, but the water was still shockingly cold.

When Mom needed a break and Dad and Grandpa were busy working on the farm, we would go "down home" to be under Grandma's watchful eye. The large farmhouse was a two-family home in which our grandparents lived in one half, and we lived in the other half until I was five. With a horse-drawn hay wagon, we moved all our belongings "up home," just a cornfield away. We suddenly went from a comfortable existence to a 100-year-old farmhouse with no indoor plumbing or insulation, surrounded by tall weeds and dilapidated outbuildings. My adult self understands the importance of owning your own place, but my five-year-old self earnestly loved and missed "down-home" with its bathtub, indoor toilet, and familiar surroundings.

But, back to spring break.... Grandma would usually let us play outdoors to our delight, but when it was mealtime, we had better hear that cowbell and run home. Most farmers ate their main meal midday, probably because they had been up since 5:00 am to milk the cows, and there was still an entire workday ahead. For Grandma, preparing that main meal and setting the table was not just a casual affair but a lengthy ritual that could take all morning. Grandma was also a meticulous homemaker, so when we ran home beet red, sweaty, and smeared with dirt, she would grin in wonderment at how incredibly filthy we could get. Of course, we had to be as neat as her table setting, so she would scrub us squeaky clean before we could sit.

Along with Dad and Grandpa at the table and the four of us, hired hands who helped with haying or filling silos joined us. Sometimes, even our pastor would stop by for a meal. He was always welcome since Grandma could easily fit ten at her large kitchen table. Until I got older, I thought everyone enjoyed a noontime meal consisting of enormous platters of meat and potatoes, homegrown vegetables, and fresh bread and butter at a table set to perfection!

Just as Grandma did, I often include small bowls of cottage cheese and applesauce and, of course, a tray of pickles and olives for garnish. I also learned how to dress up a table with glassware, china, silverware, a pretty tablecloth, and festive centerpiece. Although we no longer eat a farmer's big midday meal, I realize that I have adopted many of Grandma's customs and, hopefully, added more of my own to be handed down to my children and grandchildren.

Grandma and Grandpa Loomis on
Their 40th Wedding Anniversary

Acknowledgments

I am grateful to my publisher, Jeanne Johansen, for believing in this project from the beginning and throughout the four years I struggled with the decision to make my story public.

I thank the Williamsburg, Virginia Critique Group members who read most of the original manuscript and offered valuable suggestions.

I wish to thank Dr. Beverly Peterson, my first beta reader, Ann Eichenmuller, who edited the initial draft, and my poet friend, Sharon Dorsey, who helped me with the poem, "Ode to My Parents." Each of them encouraged me to continue when I thought of giving up.

I gratefully acknowledge The Waterville, New York Historical Society for permission to use the photographs in Chapter 14, and I am grateful to my beloved sister-in-law, Sandy Forbes Loomis, for painstakingly organizing and distributing Mom's collection of family pictures.

I thank my beta readers, who kindly reviewed the finished memoir, each providing wisdom and encouragement: the amazing author, Dr. Scott Butler, and my cherished friend of more than thirty years, Tamara Carver.

As always, I am grateful to my long-suffering husband, Carl, who puts up with my closed door and extended periods of silence whenever I'm writing.

Author Biography

 Cindy L. Freeman began earnest writing after retiring from a long career in music education and music ministry. A published author of novels, blogs, and award-winning essays, she also edits for High Tide Publications. In her novels, she tackles sensitive social issues where strong women find the courage to overcome adversity.

Cindy serves on the Writers Guild of Virginia Board as editor of the organization's literary journal and monthly newsletter. She lives in James City County, Virginia with her husband, Carl, with whom she has co-written, under duress, the first science-fiction novel of a trilogy, *Krell Domus: Katerina*. They have two amazing children, five favorite grandchildren, and numerous granddogs and grandhorses.

To learn more, visit her:

Website at http://www.cindylfreeman.com,

Facebook page: https://www.facebook.com/cindy.l.freeman.9, or

Blog site: www.cindylfreeman.blogspot.com

Other Books by Cindy L. Freeman

Unrevealed

The Dark Room

I Want to Go Home

After Rain

**Available from Amazon or
High Tide Publications, Inc.
www.hightidepublications.com**

If you enjoyed this book, please consider leaving a review on Amazon.com.

Thank you for your support.

Made in the USA
Middletown, DE
28 April 2023

29608410R00086